MENTAL HEALTH MATTERS

UNDERSTANDING SUBSTANCE USE DISORDERS

SIMON PIERCE

ROSEN PUBLISHING

Published in 2026 by The Rosen Publishing Group, Inc.
2544 Clinton Street, Buffalo, NY 14224

Portions of this work were originally authored by Nicole Horning and published as *Drug Addiction and Substance Use Disorders*. All new material this edition authored by Simon Pierce.

Cataloging-in-Publication Data

Names: Pierce, Simon.
Title: Understanding substance use disorders / Simon Pierce.
Description: First edition. | Buffalo, NY : Rosen Publishing, 2026. | Series: Mental health matters | Includes glossary and index.
Identifiers: ISBN 9781499479690 (pbk.) | ISBN 9781499479706 (library bound) | ISBN 9781499479713 (ebook)
Subjects: LCSH: Substance abuse--Juvenile literature. | Substance abuse--Diagnosis--Juvenile literature.| Substance abuse--Treatment--Juvenile literature.
Classification: LCC RC564.3 P55 2026 | DDC 362.29--dc23

Manufactured in the United States of America

CPSIA Compliance Information: Batch #CSRYA26. For further information, contact Rosen Publishing at 1-800-237-9932.

CONTENTS

FOREWORD 4

INTRODUCTION
A MISUNDERSTOOD DISEASE 6

CHAPTER ONE
ADDICTIVE SUBSTANCES 11

CHAPTER TWO
A DEEPER UNDERSTANDING 41

CHAPTER THREE
LIVING WITH SUBSTANCE ABUSE 52

CHAPTER FOUR
TREATMENT OPTIONS 62

CHAPTER FIVE
ADDRESSING THE PROBLEM 73

NOTES 85
GLOSSARY 91
ORGANIZATIONS TO CONTACT 93
FOR MORE INFORMATION 95
INDEX 97
PHOTO CREDITS 103
ABOUT THE AUTHOR 104

FOREWORD

There are many misconceptions about illness, especially mental illness. Advances in scientific knowledge have increased our understanding of many diseases and disorders, including the common cold, diabetes, and cancer. Many of these sicknesses and chronic conditions cause physical symptoms that people can see and understand, and their causes are often easy to explain.

The same cannot always be said for mental illnesses. Mental disorders are just as common as physical disorders, but without physical symptoms, they are often dismissed. People tend to believe that a mental illness is easy to get over with enough willpower. They may call people with mental illnesses names such as "lazy" and "attention-seeking." Some people even deny that mental illnesses exist at all.

People who have been convinced by those around them that they have a problem of willpower rather than a treatable illness often go undiagnosed for years. This can cause a lot of suffering; people with an undiagnosed mental disorder often understand that they are experiencing the world in a different way than their peers, but they have no one to turn to for answers. Many feel guilty about not being able to control their symptoms, not realizing that this is as impractical as telling someone with a broken leg that they should be able to walk without pain if they simply try hard enough.

In recent years, the stigma, or perceived shame, of mental illness has decreased. More people, especially young people, are willing to seek therapy and talk openly about their diagnosed mental illnesses. However, this has also led to a rise in misinformation, which can be spread through personal anecdotes, social media, and even news sources. The misuse of "therapy speak" and armchair diagnoses by internet commenters are two growing problems. Furthermore, although the stigma has lessened, it has not disappeared completely. People sometimes use mental illnesses as insults. Someone who displays normal ranges of emotion, for example, may be called "bipolar" as an insult. This shows a lack of understanding about bipolar disorder and furthers the stigma around this disorder by making it sound like a negative aspect of who a person is.

This series aims to offer accurate information about mental illnesses so young adults will have a better understanding of them. Each volume discusses the symptoms of a particular illness, ways it is currently being treated, and the research that is being done to understand it further. Advice for people who may be suffering from a disorder is included, as well as information for their loved ones about how best to support them.

With fully cited quotes, a list of recommended books and websites for further research, and informational charts, this series provides young adults with a factual introduction to common mental illnesses. By learning more about these disorders, they will be better able to show compassion to people who are dealing with mental illnesses and take charge of their own mental health.

INTRODUCTION

A MISUNDERSTOOD DISEASE

Substance use disorders are extremely common worldwide. Many substances, including illegal drugs, prescription medications, and alcohol have the potential to create an addiction in the person using them. Whether someone is suffering from a substance use disorder themselves or knows someone who is, the impact of these disorders is quite large. However, even with so many people being affected by a substance use disorder in some way, there is still a stigma, or negative view, surrounding this issue. As the National Institute on Drug Abuse (NIDA) wrote:

> *Many people don't understand why or how other people become addicted to drugs. They may mistakenly think that those who use drugs lack moral principles or willpower and that they could stop their drug use simply by choosing to. In reality, drug addiction is a complex disease, and quitting usually takes more than good intentions or a strong will. Drugs change the brain in ways that make quitting hard, even for those who want to.*[1]

Substance use disorders are chronic disorders that are hard to control; even though the person

When a person has a substance use disorder, they often feel as though that substance rules their life. They struggle to stop using it even when they want to.

may know that what they are doing is harmful to them, drugs and alcohol hijack the brain in a way that makes it hard to resist them.

IMPORTANT TERMS

Generally, the initial decision to try a drug is voluntary. However, the euphoric feeling the drug provides affects the reward circuit in the brain, and the person may continue to use the drug to achieve that same euphoric feeling, which is known as a high. For other people, an addiction may develop from legally prescribed drugs such as opioids. Although they start out taking them for a legitimate ailment, the person may, over time, need increasingly higher doses to achieve the same effect. This is called developing a tolerance, and it is especially common with drugs such as cocaine and heroin. People who develop a

Cigarettes are very addictive and also very harmful to a person's health, but false advertising in the past made them seem safe and fun. Smoking indoors in places such as bars and restaurants was common in many parts of the world through the mid-2000s, despite the fact that even secondhand smoke poses health risks.

tolerance to a drug frequently also develop a dependency on it, which means their body (if it is a physical dependency) or their brain (if it is a psychological dependency) craves the drug and does not feel normal without it. A dependency becomes an addiction when someone is unable to go without the drug, even when using it starts to interfere negatively with their life.

It is important for people to understand the language used to talk about substance use disorders because it can help frame these disorders as serious medical conditions rather than moral failings. For example, relapse—turning back to drug use—is common during treatment. However, that does not mean that the treatment or the person failed. Saying they failed may drive the person struggling with a substance use disorder even more toward drugs or alcohol in an effort to make themselves feel better.

MAKING A PLAN

There are a number of risk factors contributing to the development of a substance use disorder. The environment a person is in can greatly affect their decision to use drugs—for example, if they have suffered past trauma, such as abuse, or if the person is homeless.

Like other chronic disorders, such as asthma or diabetes, a substance use disorder cannot be completely cured. It can be treated and managed successfully, but there will be a risk of relapse for years—possibly even the rest of the person's life. This constant risk of relapse is why it is especially important for the individual to have a treatment plan that works for them. As NIDA wrote, "Treatment approaches tailored to each patient's drug use patterns and any co-occurring medical, mental, and social problems can lead to continued recovery."[2]

The addictive nature of many drugs and the fact that, at a certain point, a person with a substance use disorder has limited or no control over their ability to resist the substance makes a compassionate and educated approach important. A person with a substance use disorder needs to be seen as a human who has a medical condition rather than someone who has deliberately tried to hurt themselves and their loved ones. This is why understanding the science behind addiction is key to helping people with substance use disorders successfully establish a clean and sober way of life.

ADDICTIVE SUBSTANCES

There are many different types of addictive substances, but not all are equally addictive or equally destructive. For example, heroin and cocaine are highly addictive and easy to abuse, but cannabis has a very low risk for addiction. One of the keys to reducing the stigma surrounding substance use disorders and understanding what a person with one is going through is to learn the facts about addictive substances and the pull they can have on a person.

AN ACCEPTED SUBSTANCE

Alcohol is frequently not thought of as a drug, partially because it is not only legal but generally celebrated. Many cultures around the world have customs tied to certain alcoholic drinks, and bars are a common meeting place for adults. It is considered completely normal to have a drink a few times a week; in fact, people who choose not to drink alcohol are sometimes questioned about why they are not drinking. However, such attitudes mask the danger of alcohol. It can alter the way a person behaves, and for about 6 percent of the population, it is extremly addictive. Additionally, even without an addiction, drinking too much on a consistent basis can take a toll on a person's health—sometimes permanently.

The drinking of alcoholic beverages goes back thousands of years. The Chinese made a type of wine from fruit, honey, and rice 9,000 years ago. Grape wine started to be made about 8,000 years ago, after people learned how to grow their own grapes. Alcohol of all types was seen as an important part of people's diets, especially before water purification systems were invented. In the 1600s, when English colonists sailed to Massachusetts Bay in North America, there was more beer than water on the ship. Small amounts of alcohol would be drunk throughout the day, with the average American in the 1790s consuming an average of 5.8 gallons (22 liters) of alcohol a year. According to Bruce Bustard, curator of a 2015 exhibit at the U.S. National Archives called *Spirited Republic: Alcohol in American History*, "We think of that as an astounding amount—you would think people would be staggering around drunk, but most people were able to handle their alcohol because it was integrated into daily life."[3]

From 1920 to 1933, the United States banned the sale of alcohol. However, this did not stop people from drinking in secret bars known as speakeasies. These were sometimes hidden behind elevators.

This common use of alcohol means it has generally been seen as a more acceptable substance than other drugs. This acceptability of alcohol also means young people may feel like it is an acceptable substance to experiment with, even though it is illegal for anyone under 21 to purchase alcohol in the United States. According to the 2023 National Survey on Drug Use and Health, 5.6 million Americans ages 12 to 20 have had more than just a few sips of alcohol. While this is a lot, it is a decrease from the numbers reflected in the 2017 version of the study. In fact, rising numbers of young people are turning away from alcohol completely in recent years.

Although alcohol is a commonly used substance, that does not mean it is inherently safe or without negative consequences. *National Geographic* explained how alcohol affects the brain, which contributes to a person developing an alcohol use disorder:

> *The active ingredient common to all alcoholic beverages is made by yeasts: microscopic, single-celled organisms that eat sugar and excrete carbon dioxide and ethanol, the only [drinkable] alcohol ... From our modern point of view, ethanol has one very compelling property: It makes us feel good. Ethanol helps release serotonin, dopamine, and endorphins in the brain, chemicals that make us happy and less anxious.*[4]

Alcohol is generally categorized by the type of process it undergoes when it is made—distillation or fermentation. Fermented beverages include beer, wine, and hard cider. Distilled beverages include liquors such as vodka, rum, gin, whiskey, tequila, and brandy. Fermentation can only take the alcohol content to a certain point; after that, to get a higher alcohol content, the liquid needs to be distilled. The distillation process involves "separating the alcohol in a fermented brew from its separate parts ... By separating the alcohol from the rest, it will become much more concentrated."[5] These distilled liquors are often used in mixed drinks with soda or juice. Mixing liquor and a sweet beverage such as a juice generally makes the mixed drink taste better because it masks the taste of the alcohol. However, this makes it much easier for someone to unintentionally get drunk because they cannot judge by taste how much alcohol they are drinking. While most bars have set amounts of liquor in their drinks, some bartenders are "heavy pourers" and may put more liquor into one drink than another. Additionally, when people are mixing their own drinks, they may not measure out their alcohol at all.

Alcohol affects each person differently. Depending on factors such as a person's height, weight, body fat percentage, and whether they have eaten recently, it may take three drinks for one person to feel the effects, while for others, it may

Bars are common places for people to gather. Although a person can be in one with friends and not be drinking, it can be difficult for someone who does not want to drink to be in a bar.

only take one. As someone drinks more frequently, their tolerance to alcohol builds, and then they need more and more to get drunk.

As a person has more drinks throughout a night, the effects of the alcohol and the risks associated with them multiply, and they last for several hours after the person stops drinking. They include:

- ***Inhibitions and memory:*** *People may say and do things that they will regret later, or possibly not remember at all. Inhibitions are lost—leading to poor decision making.*
- ***Decision-making skills:*** *When they drink, individuals are more likely to be impulsive. They may be at a greater risk for having an alcohol-related traffic crash, getting into fights, or making unwise decisions …*
- ***Coordination and physical control:*** *When drinking leads to loss of balance, slurred speech, and blurred vision, even normal activities can become more dangerous.*
- ***Death:*** *Drinking too much alcohol can also lead to death. If people drink too much, they will eventually get sleepy and pass out. Reflexes like gagging and breathing can be suppressed. That means they could vomit and choke, or stop breathing completely.*[6]

CANNABIS

One of the most commonly used drugs in the United States is cannabis, also known as marijuana or weed. While the rates of cannabis use among middle school and high school students have decreased, students today still tend to underestimate the risks associated with cannabis use. A number of factors may contribute to this, including the rising acceptability of cannabis for medicinal use and the legalization of the drug in some states.

The chemical responsible for the majority of cannabis's effects is tetrahydrocannabinol (THC).

ALCOHOL AND DRUGS DON'T MIX

Alcohol is a depressant, which means it slows down the central nervous system. Combining alcohol with other drugs can cause dangerous effects and put the body at risk, no matter what type of drug it is. If alcohol is combined with another depressant such as heroin, the central nervous system will be extremely slowed down, doubling the risk of the body shutting down completely.

If alcohol is combined with a stimulant such as cocaine, the depressant effect of the alcohol will try to slow the body systems down while the stimulant will try to speed it up. The conflicting effects of these two drugs put a lot of strain on the central nervous system, and the stimulant can "conceal alcohol's effects, so people cannot gauge their level of intoxication, which can result in over-consumption, e.g. significant impairment of coordination and judgment, black out, pass out and potential death."[1]

Combining cocaine and alcohol can also create an entirely new substance called cocaethylene. This substance is produced in the liver and "causes the highest level of cardiovascular activity of any drug, which puts extreme pressure and stress on the heart and often leads to cardiac arrest and death."[2] Cocaethylene is 30 percent more toxic than cocaine, and "once the liver begins producing it, the chemical keeps being released in the system and remains in the body up to three times longer than cocaine, resulting in increased potential for toxic effects."[3] Cocaethylene can get into a person's bloodstream, and once this happens, it can have a serious effect on their cardiovascular system, which is the body system that includes the heart.

Alcohol is also dangerous when it is combined with many different kinds of prescription drugs. Just because prescription drugs are legal, that does not mean they are safe to mix with alcohol.

1. "The Effects of Combining Alcohol with Other Drugs," University of Michigan, accessed on September 26, 2018. uhs.umich.edu/combine.

2. Jeffrey Juergens, "Mixing Alcohol and Other Substances," Addiction Center, last updated January 4, 2019. www.addictioncenter.com/alcohol/mixing-alcohol-drugs/.

3. "Cocaethylene Effects and Dangers: The Product of Cocaine and Alcohol Use," American Addiction Centers, last updated November 26, 2018. americanaddictioncenters.org/alcoholism-treatment/mixing-cocaine-and-alcohol/.

According to NIDA:

> *[THC] acts much like the cannabinoid chemicals made naturally by the body … Cannabinoid receptors are concentrated in certain areas of the brain associated with thinking, memory, pleasure, coordination and time perception. THC attaches to these receptors and activates them and affects a person's memory, pleasure, movements, thinking, concentration, coordination, and sensory and time perception.*[7]

The effects of cannabis start to be felt about 15 to 30 minutes after it is smoked. It may take longer—up to two or three hours—to feel the effects when someone consumes edibles, or food made with cannabis, but the effects last longer and are more intense. THC then makes the brain release dopamine, which causes the user to feel high. Other effects may include a change in mood, difficulty with problem solving, hallucinations, and a change in senses.

Throughout the past few decades, the amount of THC in cannabis has increased, which means there is more of a chance that someone will have a harmful reaction. In the 1970s, THC levels in cannabis were at only 1 percent, but due to selective breeding of cannabis plants, they have risen to more than 30 percent in some plants. This increase in THC is one of the factors that make it difficult for researchers to determine the long-term effects of cannabis.

Additionally, not all strains of cannabis have the same amount of THC in them, and unless they are labeled—as they would be in a legal shop called a dispensary that has tested for THC content—it is impossible for someone to tell how much is in each plant. This can also be a problem when cannabis is baked into food. Because it takes longer for the effects to be felt with edibles, someone may eat too much at one time, thinking they got a strain with a low THC content. Then, when it all kicks in at once, the effects can be too intense and, depending on the situation, very dangerous. For example, if someone eats several cannabis brownies, leaves their friend's house, and then experiences the effects while driving home, their driving will be impaired, and they have a high risk of hurting or killing themselves and others.

Although cannabis can have dangerous results if too much is ingested, a person cannot fatally overdose on cannabis. An overdose occurs when someone takes too much of a drug or combination of drugs; generally, this results in dangerous—sometimes deadly—symptoms. People who ingest more cannabis than they can handle may feel some uncomfortable side effects, such as paranoia, but there is no evidence that cannabis alone can cause a fatal overdose.

The question of whether cannabis is addictive is a controversial one. Some people believe it is impossible to develop a cannabis use disorder, but studies have proven this false. The legalization of cannabis across the United States and in countries such as Canada has increased the availability and marketing of the product, but experts say the addiction rate has stayed relatively level. About 10 percent of all users develop some degree of cannabis use disorder, but for those who start using it when they are teenagers, that number is four to seven times greater. However, according to NIDA, these numbers are somewhat controversial because "studies of substance use often use dependence as a proxy for addiction even though it is possible to be dependent without being addicted."[8] Although the numbers may be slightly lower, experts agree that cannabis use disorder is a very real issue, but only about 5 percent of people who experience it get the treatment they need—partially because so few people admit that this disorder is real.

One of the concerns people have about legalized cannabis sellers is that some employees working in these stores are not licensed or trained medical professionals but are still giving medical advice regarding cannabis use. This can be quite dangerous for the person buying the product when the person giving the advice does not know the buyer's medical history. Another concern of health experts is that legalized cannabis is not highly regulated but is widely available. Stemming off of this concern is the belief that heavy users of cannabis will be the ones to make up the largest share of sales and the fear that businesses will take advantage of this and encourage them to buy more, spend more, and use more of the drug regardless of what the consequences to the user are.

Kevin Sabet, founder of the nonprofit organization Smart Approaches to Cannabis, told *The Atlantic* in August 2018, "The reckless way that we are legalizing cannabis so far is mind-boggling from a public-health perspective ... The issue now is that we have lobbyists, special interests, and people whose motivation is to make money that are writing all of these laws and taking control of the conversation."[9]

CANNABIS AS A TREATMENT

In addition to recreational use, cannabis is also being legalized for medical use. As of early 2025, 40 states and Washington, D.C., have legalized cannabis to some degree. Washington, D.C., and 24 states have full legalization, meaning people are allowed to use it either for recreational or medical

Due to the legalization of cannabis, many states now have legal cannabis farms.

purposes. The other 16 states have legalized it for medical purposes only. Some states have decriminalized cannabis, which means individuals who are found with small amounts of the drug on them will not be arrested or fined, but large-scale trafficking organizations will still be targeted. Finally, some states still have not legalized or decriminalized cannabis to any degree.

Cannabis does not cure any medical condition, but it is often used in a variety of forms to treat nausea, loss of appetite, post-traumatic stress disorder (PTSD), multiple sclerosis, chronic pain, anxiety disorders, and inflammatory bowel disease. However, the *Journal of the American Medical Association* "found little evidence for cannabis's ability to treat health conditions outside [of] chronic pain, chemotherapy-induced nausea and vomiting, and ... multiple sclerosis."[10]

There have not been many studies on cannabis's effectiveness as a medicine. This is because of how much it has historically been restricted by the U.S. government. Even though cannabis has been legalized in many states, it is still listed as a Schedule I drug by the U.S. Drug Enforcement Administration (DEA), which means it is illegal at the federal level. Crossing state lines with cannabis products can be grounds for an arrest if the person is caught.

Schedule I is the level shared by drugs such as heroin and lysergic acid diethylamide (LSD). Schedule I drugs "are defined as drugs with no currently accepted medical use and a high potential for abuse."[11] Cannabis is even listed higher on the DEA drug schedules than cocaine, which is a Schedule II drug. Schedule I drugs are the most tightly restricted, and until cannabis started to be legalized by states, researchers needed special permission from the government to do legal studies on it. In 2024, the federal government announced that it would reclassify cannabis as a Schedule III drug, which means it would still be restricted but would be considered to have a lower risk of addiction. As of 2025, this change has not been made.

In addition to helping treat symptoms of disorders such as epilepsy, several studies have shown

LAB-MADE CANNABINOIDS

Synthetic cannabinoids are made by spraying harmless plants with chemicals that were made in a lab to mimic the effects of cannabis. They were originally designed by scientists for research purposes, but when the methods of how they were produced were published in scientific journals, people began recreating the methods themselves for recreational purposes. Today, synthetic cannabinoids are sold under a variety of names, but the most common are K2 and Spice.

While K2 and Spice have frequently been labeled as "fake cannabis" or "legal weed," the label is misleading. Cannabis is grown, whereas the chemicals in K2 and Spice are man-made. This makes it hard to know what other ingredients have been added—it can be one additional chemical, or it can be a mixture of various chemicals. Additionally, these labels can lead people to trust these drugs and think they will act like real cannabis. However, this is a false belief, as toxic chemicals can be added to the drug, and the effects are sometimes much different, stronger, and more dangerous than those of cannabis. Furthermore, unlike natural cannabis, fatal or near-fatal overdoses on synthetic cannabinoids are common. Side effects of K2 and Spice include:

- *Racing heart*
- *Agitation and anxiety*
- *Paranoia*
- *Hallucinations—seeing or hearing things that aren't real*
- *Psychosis—loss of touch with reality*
- *High blood pressure*
- *Shortness of breath*
- *Chest pain*
- *Seizures*
- *Nausea and vomiting*[1]

that cannabis can also help address the crisis of opioid addiction and overdoses. These studies suggest that

> *legalizing medical cannabis dispensaries can lead to fewer opioid painkiller deaths, making medical cannabis one potential way to help fight the opioid epidemic. The rationale for this is simple: Studies show cannabis can effectively*

Between March and June of 2018, synthetic cannabinoids were associated with more than 160 instances of severe bleeding and four deaths in Illinois. Within a two-day period in August 2018, more than 100 people overdosed on synthetic cannabinoids in New Haven, Connecticut.

The active ingredient in K2 and Spice is sprayed on dried plant material, such as herbs. The plant material is then smoked the same way cannabis would be.

1. Stephanie Watson, "K2/Spice: What to Know About These Dangerous Drugs," WebMD, September 10, 2018. www.webmd.com/mental-health/addiction/news/20180910/k2-spice-what-to-know-about-these-dangerous-drugs.

> *treat chronic pain, which opioids are commonly used for. But unlike opioids, medical cannabis cannot cause deadly overdoses. So medical cannabis could supplant some opioid use and* save *some lives.*[12]

Considering the high addiction potential of opioids and the fact that more than 200 people in the United States die each day from opioid overdoses, this is something many people are interested in pursuing. In July 2018, the New York State Department of Health added regulations stating that if a person had a condition that could allow them to receive a prescription for an opioid medication, that condition could be a qualifying condition for medical cannabis, thus replacing the highly addictive opioid medication with a drug that so far has been shown to have a much lower addiction risk.

TOBACCO PRODUCTS

Another drug that is legal—and has been for decades—is nicotine. This chemical is a natural product of several plants, including tobacco. It can also be produced synthetically, or in a lab. It can be found in products such as cigarettes, vapes, chewing tobacco, gum, nasal spray, and patches that are applied to the skin. Products that include only nicotine and no tobacco are typically intended to be used as a way to help someone quit using tobacco products. Nicotine is a highly addictive drug; according to *Medical News Today*, it is as hard to quit as heroin.

When the body is exposed to nicotine, its first reaction is a minor high caused by the drug's stimulation of the user's adrenal glands. This causes an increase in blood pressure and a spike in adrenaline, which is a hormone that makes people feel more awake and alert. Nicotine also stimulates the areas of the brain related to pleasure and motivation, which is similar to what happens when someone takes drugs such as cocaine or heroin. These pleasant feelings are what create the addiction. Nicotine can also have negative side effects on the heart, hormones, and digestive system.

It is commonly known that cigarettes have incredibly harmful effects; for example, they have been proven many times over to cause various kinds of cancer as well as diseases of the heart, lungs, and other organs. According to the Centers for Disease Control and Prevention (CDC), more than 480,000 Americans die each year due to ciga-

Vape pens have cartridges that can be swapped out. They come in many different flavors, which increases the appeal of smoking and masks the health risks vaping poses.

rette use. However, while nicotine is the substance that gets someone addicted to cigarettes, it is the tar, lead, and other dangerous chemicals added to tobacco products that cause cancer. Nicotine on its own has not been shown to cause cancer. In fact, some studies suggest that it can improve memory and concentration and may help treat some neurological diseases, such as Parkinson's disease and schizophrenia (a mental illness characterized by delusions and hallucinations). For this reason, some researchers are trying to see if it can be scientifically proven that nicotine does have such benefits. If the researchers discover that nicotine can be helpful, "clean" forms of nicotine such as gum or patches may be available by prescription in the future. In the meantime, experts strongly caution people not to smoke cigarettes or use other tobacco products, as the risks associated with them are so high that they negate any small benefit someone might get from the nicotine in them.

In recent years, smoking e-cigarettes, or vaping, has risen in popularity, as it has been marketed as a "healthy" alternative to smoking traditional cigarettes. Vaping is also attractive to many people because the cartridges are available in a wide range of flavors. Experts say that vaping is a less harmful way to smoke because the cartridges contain fewer than the 7,000 chemicals that exist in traditional cigarettes. However, different vape brands have different chemical formulas that they keep private, making it difficult to know exactly what chemicals someone is consuming when they vape. Furthermore, just because vaping is less harmful does not mean that it is completely harmless. When people vape frequently, they are taking in high doses of nicotine as well as toxic chemicals and heavy metals. Even brands that are labeled nicotine-free have been found to have small amounts of nicotine in them. The effects of nicotine, especially in high doses, on a person's blood pressure and adrenaline can increase the risk of having a heart attack. Medical experts say there is no doubt that vaping has serious negative effects on health and is just as addictive as smoking.

Many people are skeptical about the health risks nicotine poses because cigarettes and vape pens are legal. If it were so dangerous, they say, the government would not allow these items to be sold. In reality, the continued sale of tobacco products is deeply rooted in economics and politics. Tobacco company executives were aware as early as the 1950s that their products were harmful, but through aggressive and sustained ad campaigns, they managed to hide this fact for several more decades.

Today, the U.S. government has tried virtually everything to discourage people from smoking—including printing warnings and unpleasant pictures on cigarette cartons, raising the price to make cigarettes harder for people to afford, and requiring stores to keep cigarettes out of sight instead of on display—except for outright banning tobacco products. Most of these efforts have been met with resistance from tobacco companies and smokers alike, so politicians know that they would lose many smokers' votes if they proposed banning cigarettes and vape pens.

Additionally, thousands of people are employed by tobacco companies, so banning tobacco products would cause serious problems for the American economy if they were shut down overnight. Since it is unlikely tobacco products will be discontinued any time soon, it is up to consumers to use their common sense and avoid this very dangerous and highly addictive substance.

NATURAL OPIOIDS

The opium poppy flower is the source of several natural opioids, including opium, heroin, and morphine. Three months after the poppy flower seeds are planted, the bright petals bloom and eventually fall away, revealing an egg-shaped pod. Once the pod is revealed, a farmer makes vertical cuts around the pod. Milky opium sap oozes out of these cuts, and "as the sap oozes out, it turns darker and thicker, forming a brownish-black gum. A farmer collects the gum with a scraping knife, bundles it into bricks, cakes or balls and wraps them in a simple material such as plastic or leaves."[13] Once the opium arrives at a refinery, it is mixed in boiling water with lime—a chemical made from burned and powdered limestone, not to be confused with the harmless citrus fruit—and then the waste sinks to the bottom while "on the surface a white band of morphine forms. This is drawn off, reheated with ammonia, filtered and boiled again until it is reduced to a brown paste."[14] This paste is dried in the sun until it has the consistency of clay, and then equal amounts of the morphine paste and other chemicals are heated in a container. From this point, the mixture is repeatedly drained, filtered, and purified until the heroin powder is left.

The color and style of heroin can vary greatly between a fluffy white powder and a sticky black substance that is known as "black tar heroin." The color depends on impurities in the manufacturing process and whether additional materials such as sugar were added to the powder as a filler.

Opium was frequently used in the past as a medicine, until its potential for addiction was discovered. Morphine is still frequently used under careful supervision, such as in hospitals after major surgery. Heroin is not used for medical purposes, but it is commonly used for recreational purposes. Heroin can be inhaled, smoked, or injected. Injection delivers the quickest and most dangerous response—within seconds, the user feels the effects. It is easier to overdose while injecting heroin than inhaling or smoking. When inhaled, it is about 10 to 15 minutes before effects are felt. At that point, it delivers an intense feeling of happiness that some users have said is like being "covered in a warm blanket, where worries are gone."[15] This feeling is generally the reason people use the drug, eventually leading them to become addicted to it.

Along with this intense euphoric feeling, heroin slows things down. The user feels like they have no problems, their limbs feel heavy, and they also feel relaxed and tired. This effect is what is commonly referred to as being "on the nod." However, heroin also slows down important body functions such as heart rate and breathing. This becomes especially dangerous if the user falls asleep. People's breathing naturally gets slower when they fall asleep, so combined with the effects of heroin, the respiratory system may stop altogether. According to Dr. Karen Drexler, "when you are sleeping, your body naturally remembers to breathe. In the case of a heroin overdose, you fall asleep and essentially your body forgets."[16]

Heroin has equally dangerous long-term effects. The respiratory and circulatory systems are affected by chronic use, and heart infections and lung complications may result from extended use.

Additionally, heroin may be cut with dangerous or unknown additives. Cutting heroin with fillers

CUT WITH FENTANYL

Drugs can be cut with anything without the buyer's knowledge. Therefore, a person might buy something that is much more powerful than they were expecting it to be, which can be deadly. Additionally, they are unable to predict what kinds of interactions might happen between the various drugs they are taking without knowing exactly what is in the mix. In 2018, when singer Demi Lovato was taken to the hospital for an overdose, it was reported that the oxycodone she bought from her drug dealer had been cut with fentanyl, which made it stronger.

It is becoming increasingly common for drugs to be cut with fentanyl because fentanyl is much cheaper and easier to synthesize, or make in a lab. When the fentanyl is powdered, it can look just like heroin or cocaine, so the dealer can increase their profits by selling someone cheap fentanyl for expensive cocaine prices.

Drug dealers have also been known to sell fentanyl disguised as weaker prescription pills such as oxycodone. This is especially harmful for first-time users because their system has no tolerances built up, so even a small amount can cause a fatal overdose.

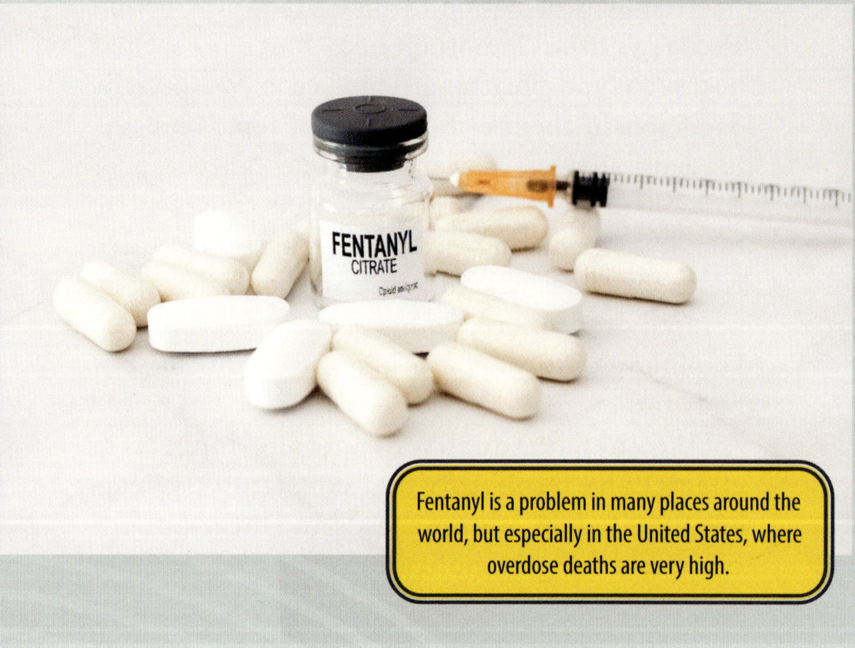

Fentanyl is a problem in many places around the world, but especially in the United States, where overdose deaths are very high.

such as baby powder, cornstarch, shoe polish, dirt, or strychnine (a chemical used in rat poison) helps dealers stretch out a batch of heroin and increase their profits. These additives may clog the blood vessels that lead to organs such as the lungs or liver, which in turn may cause infection or cell death.

The method of using heroin also has risks for the user. For example, if the user prefers to inhale heroin repeatedly, tissues in the nose can become damaged. Another consequence of inhaling heroin is a perforated septum. The septum is the delicate bone and cartilage structure that separates the nostrils. With repeated inhalation of toxic substances, "the cartilage begins to die, and a hole develops."[17] This hole can cause "whistling, nosebleeds ... infections, nasal congestion, sinusitis, and nasal collapse deformity."[18] When there is nasal collapse, the nostrils can close to small slits and make it difficult to breathe. These problems can cause massive amounts of damage that require challenging surgeries and recovery time.

SYNTHETIC OPIOIDS

Some legal prescription drugs, such as oxycodone (OxyContin), hydrocodone (Vicodin), and fentanyl, have the same chemical makeup as the drugs that come from the opium poppy, but are synthetic. This means they are made in a medical lab. Opioids are approved for the treatment of severe pain that cannot be soothed by weaker drugs. However, fentanyl in particular is also illicitly manufactured and sold by drug dealers because it has effects similar to heroin. Additionally, fentanyl can be mixed with cocaine or heroin—often without the user's knowledge—to increase the effects of the drug. Because fentanyl is 50 to 100 times stronger than morphine, this drug combination is highly dangerous and often deadly because of how much more it depresses important body systems.

Prescription opioids are, in the opinion of many medical experts, overused. For example, some oral surgeons prescribe opioids to young adults after they have their wisdom teeth removed. While it is true that people generally feel pain and discomfort for several days after their surgery, many experts say it is not enough pain to justify using opioids, especially considering that this early exposure to opioids can increase a teen's addiction risk by anywhere from 33 to 300 percent.

The number of opioid prescriptions increased greatly starting in the 1990s, when pharmaceutical companies told doctors that prescription opioids were not addictive whatsoever. The idea of a highly effective, non-addictive type of painkiller made opioids seem like a "magic pill," so doctors started prescribing them with greater frequency, which led to widespread misuse of prescription opioids. Much later, when addiction rates rose and overdose rates started to increase, it became clear the overprescription of opioids had led to an epidemic that is still ongoing. In 2017 alone, more than 17,000 people in the United States died from prescription opioid overdoses. This number fell to about 14,700 by 2022. However, overdose deaths from fentanyl have been rising. Many people who become addicted to prescription opioids eventually turn to heroin or fentanyl.

In addition to a high risk of addiction, opioid medications also carry the risks of tolerance, dependence, and withdrawal. Withdrawal symptoms include anxiety, muscle aches, agitation, insomnia, diarrhea, vomiting, and nausea.

The opium poppy is the source of several different kinds of highly addictive drugs.

COCAINE AND CRACK

Cocaine can come in powder or rock form. The rock form is called crack for the sound it makes when it is burned. Like most drugs, cocaine produces a feeling of euphoria when taken. However, while other drugs may take as long as 30 minutes to kick in, cocaine's effects happen immediately and disappear within an hour. According to NIDA:

> *Small amounts of cocaine make the user feel euphoric, energetic, talkative, mentally alert, and hypersensitive to sight, sound, and touch. The drug can also temporarily decrease the need for food and sleep … The duration of cocaine's euphoric effects depend upon the route of administration. The faster the drug is absorbed, the more intense the resulting high, but also the shorter its duration. Snorting cocaine produces a relatively slow onset of the high, but it may last from 15 to 30 minutes. In contrast, the high from smoking is more immediate but may only last 5 to 10 minutes.*[19]

The instantaneous effect is appealing and often addictive for the drug user, but cocaine has a lot of fillers and chemicals added to the mixture that make it even more deadly. As many as 16 different chemicals can be added to the mixture. One common cocaine filler is a dental anesthetic called lidocaine, which can cause cancer if it is ingested frequently.

Cocaine is made from coca plant leaves. The leaves themselves are not dangerous; they have been used as a mild stimulant by Indigenous groups in the Andes mountains for centuries. However, the process of creating cocaine involves making the active ingredient in coca leaves more potent, or powerful.

The leaves are first soaked in gasoline to release their active ingredient. The gasoline is then combined with diluted acid. Later, the gasoline is removed from the mixture, and ammonia or sodium bicarbonate is added to make the cocaine base. The base is filtered through cloth, dried in the sun, and then dissolved in acetone, ether, or ethyl acetate. This new mixture is boiled, and additional chemicals such as hydrochloric acid are added. The excess chemicals are then removed from the cocaine solution by pressing and heating, making the final powder cocaine solution.

The long-term side effects of cocaine depend on how it is used. For example, snorting cocaine increases the risks of loss of sense of smell and nosebleeds. Injecting cocaine carries risks from using dirty needles, such as hepatitis C and human immunodeficiency virus (HIV), the virus that causes acquired immunodeficiency syndrome (AIDS)—a deadly disease that breaks down a person's immune system. Additionally, cocaine can cause heart problems, tissue death in the gut, and a perforated septum and nasal collapse. Some people rub cocaine on their teeth and gums, which can cause damage to the mouth such as rotting teeth and bleeding gums—effects that are shared by methamphetamine abuse.

METHAMPHETAMINE

Methamphetamine, or meth, is created by meth cooks with ingredients such as ephedrine and pseudoephedrine, which are both nasal decongestants found in cold medicines. Some medications at pharmacies are only available from the pharmacist or require buyers to show the cashier their ID because of their potential for abuse or for the production of meth. Meth is

U.S. DRUG OVERDOSE DEATHS, 1999-2021

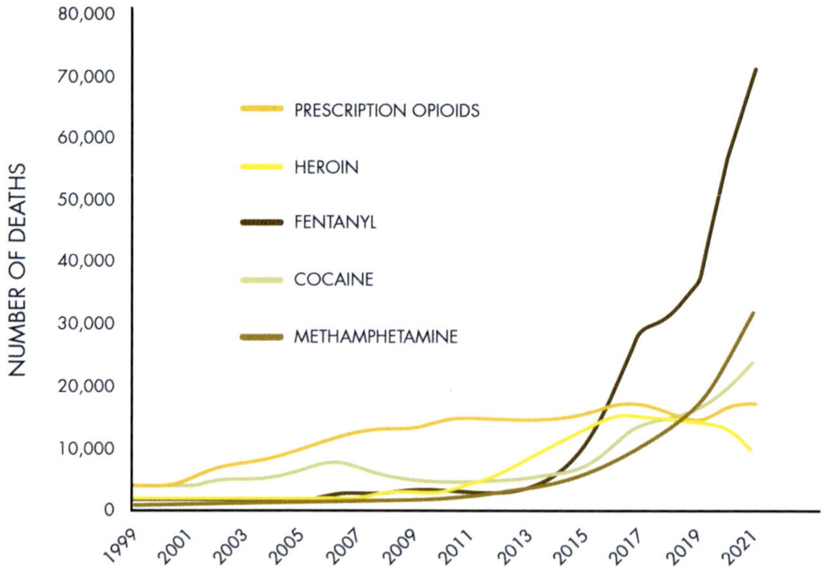

As this data from the CDC shows, fentanyl deaths have risen sharply since people started using it to cut other drugs, often without the user's knowledge.

created by combining cold medicine with chemicals such as phosphorus and hydriodic acid. This solution is then filtered through cloth and dried. With this relatively simple production method, it only takes two days to create thousands of doses. This process of making meth and the drug's short- and long-term effects were the basis of the critically acclaimed fictional television show *Breaking Bad*, in which a teacher with cancer makes and sells meth to try to earn money to support his family if he dies. The show realistically portrayed the drug's effects, including addiction.

Meth is a stimulant that, in addition to giving someone a high, generally causes an increase in attention span and activity. When someone takes the drug for an extended period of time, they may have symptoms such as confusion, anxiety, insomnia, and violent behavior. They also frequently experience paranoia and have delusions, such as imagining the feeling of insects crawling on their skin. When they try to scratch at the "insects" with fingernails or sharp objects, they hurt themselves and create a pattern of sores and scars on their skin. These take longer than normal to heal because the drug destroys blood vessels. However, an alternate theory suggests that rather than being the result of a hallucination, the imaginary bugs have a physical cause. Meth causes the body temperature to rise, making people sweat more than normal and removing protective oils from their skin. This can cause their nerve endings to tingle, resulting in this strange feeling.

Meth also causes irreversible damage to the brain. Even years after quitting meth, a user can experience episodes of paranoia and memory loss. This is due to the amount of toxic chemicals such as gasoline, phosphorus, ammonia, and even drain cleaner the person exposes their body to with repeated abuse of the drug.

While depressants slow down the body's systems, stimulants such as meth make a person more active, which may seem appealing to some people, especially when they are trying to get a lot of things done in a short amount of time. However, the dangerous chemicals that are added to the drug, its harmful side effects, and its high potential for addiction do not make this heightened energy worth it.

MDMA AND ACID

Methylenedioxymethamphetamine (MDMA), more commonly known as ecstasy or molly, is a stimulant and variation of meth. Molly is the powdered form of the drug, which is often mixed with

A FICTIONAL LINK

There is a myth that alcohol and drugs contribute to creativity, and many famous, creative people—including authors F. Scott Fitzgerald, Ernest Hemingway, and William Faulkner, musician Amy Winehouse, and actress Marilyn Monroe—have had substance use disorders. The fact that so many creative people have used various substances may lead people to think that drinking or taking drugs makes someone more creative. However, it is important to separate these people's work from their disorders; creative people do not do their best work under the influence of a substance. Psychiatrist and addiction expert Dr. Iain Smith said, "The idea that drugs and alcohol give artists unique insights and powerful experiences is an illusion … when you try and capture the experiences [triggered by drugs or alcohol], they are often nonsense."[1] Additionally, long-term, heavy use of alcohol and drugs can affect the brain negatively, with symptoms including learning problems and impaired memory—issues that can make it more difficult for someone to write or perform well.

Stephen King has written more than 50 books, many under the influence of drugs and alcohol. For a time, he feared he would be unable to write if he were sober. His family helped him overcome his addictions in the late 1980s, and he is still writing books to this day.

1. Quoted in Colleen Cancio, "Does Alcohol Affect Creativity?," HowStuffWorks, July 15, 2015. health.howstuffworks.com/wellness/drugs-alcohol/alcohol-affect-creativity.htm.

other drugs. Ecstasy is taken in pill form and the effects last up to eight hours—much longer than other drugs.

Ecstasy gives the user a feeling of emotional warmth and general well-being. Users' senses may also feel heightened. However, ecstasy also produces feelings of nausea, sweating, chills, teeth clenching, blurry vision, and muscle cramps. One of the most dangerous effects of ecstasy is a rise in body temperature, which is called hyperthermia. Hyperthermia can lead to muscle breakdown, which can result in kidney failure. Hyperthermia can also lead to dehydration and heart failure.

Ecstasy affects the same neurotransmitters—chemicals that relay messages between nerve cells—that other drugs do, but it is not as addictive as heroin or cocaine. In laboratory studies, animals have been shown to self-administer ecstasy, but they do not administer it with the frequency of some other, more addictive drugs.

Lysergic acid diethylamide (LSD or acid) is a hallucinogenic drug that does not have an odor, color, or taste. It is typically applied to small, often colorful, squares of paper that people swallow or lick. As LSD is a hallucinogen, it often causes people to say that they "see" sounds or "hear" colors, and images may be distorted. Additionally, time, space, and distance feel altered. Judgment and behavior are also affected. The experience of being under the influence of LSD is called a "trip."

LSD's effects are felt within 30 to 45 minutes and peak at around 2 to 4 hours, although they can last longer than 12 hours. As the amount of LSD ingested can vary, there is no way of knowing what kind of trip the person will have. Sometimes, a person may have what is called a "bad trip," which is often a scary, unpleasant experience with frightening hallucinations. Although LSD is not typically viewed as addictive, both this drug and ecstasy can still be taken in ways that harm a person's ability to function normally. This kind of substance use disorder is known as a hallucinogen use disorder.

Although LSD and ecstasy are labeled as Schedule I drugs by the DEA, meaning they have no official medical use, some doctors are researching the use of these drugs for the treatment of anxiety, depression, and PTSD. For example, ecstasy's effects of emotional warmth and well-being might help people with PTSD talk about the trauma that led to the development of their condition without feeling the unpleasant physical responses that generally come with reliving the event. However, just because some drugs have some medical benefits does not mean they are safe for everyone to use. Research into using recreational drugs to treat medical conditions is done under strict medical supervision to minimize bad effects, such as the risk of addiction.

A DEEPER UNDERSTANDING

Addiction is frequently misunderstood, even with the advanced knowledge medical experts have today. For instance, many people think that someone who has a substance use disorder can simply quit if they have enough willpower. However, addiction is a disease, and it does not matter if a person has a strong will. When a person develops an addiction, quitting that substance is very hard because the body and brain have become dependent on it. Treating an addiction is a difficult process that requires the understanding and support of loved ones.

A CLEAR DEFINITION

A substance use disorder is a chronic disease that is difficult to control. It is characterized by drug-seeking behaviors: Even though the person knows the substance is harmful to them, they continue to seek out and use it. Initially, for most people, the decision to try a drug is one they make themselves. However,

> *repeated drug use can lead to brain changes that challenge an addicted person's self-control and interfere with their ability to resist intense urges to take drugs. These brain changes can be persistent, which is why drug addiction is considered a "relapsing" disease—people in recovery from drug use disorders are at increased risk for returning to drug use even after years of not taking the drug.*[20]

Financial problems cause a lot of stress. This stress can lead someone to drink or use drugs to try to calm themselves. However, buying drugs then adds to a person's financial problems.

A person who is recovering from a substance use disorder can be at risk of relapsing for years—potentially even for their whole lives. While relapse is common in the recovery process of a substance use disorder, it does not mean that there is no hope for the person or that treatment does not work. Just as with many other chronic conditions, treatment needs to be ongoing and adjusted to the person's needs.

There is not one single, certain factor that means a person will end up with a substance use disorder. Rather, a combination of factors may influence the risk for addiction. Biology accounts for about half of a person's risk factors for drug addiction. Environment is another contributing factor and includes family and friends, economic status, quality of life, peer pressure, abuse, stress, and early exposure to drugs. Lastly, age is an important factor. When someone takes drugs at an early age, there is an increased risk of addiction later in life.

YOUR BRAIN ON DRUGS

The brain is composed of millions of cells called neurons. Each neuron emits an electrical impulse that carries the brain's messages, such as instructing a foot to take a step. Each neuron has a series of stems that act as pathways for the impulses. The larger stems are axons; at the end of the axons are smaller stems called axon terminals. The impulse travels along the axon to the axon terminal. When the impulse reaches the axon terminal, it must leap over a tiny space called a synapse on its way to the next neuron's dendrite, or the part that receives messages. To enable the electrical impulse to make the leap, the brain produces chemicals known as neurotransmitters, which carry the messages between the brain cells. Drugs affect neurotransmitters in ways that disrupt their normal behavior.

The brain is wired to reward people for certain behaviors by making them feel good. However, just because something feels good does not mean it is good for the person. Addictive drugs target the brain's reward center, called the basal ganglia, flooding the brain with the neurotransmitter dopamine, which causes feelings of pleasure and happiness. However, with repeated drug use, the brain adapts to the drug's presence and releases less dopamine. This is what causes someone to develop a tolerance and, eventually, an addiction: Over time, the brain comes to rely on the pleasurable sensations provided by a drug or drugs. This creates a craving in the user for larger and more frequent doses because their brain can no longer produce enough dopamine on its own.

As a person increases their use of drugs, the way

A MENTAL DISORDER

A substance use disorder is considered a disease because drugs and alcohol change the brain in ways that make it difficult or impossible for someone to stop using the substance without treatment.

The amygdala is a structure in the brain that plays a large role in processing emotions. When the brain releases dopamine while someone is under the influence of a substance, the amygdala processes the dopamine and associates the substance with reward. The extended amygdala is also affected by drug use. This area of the brain, which includes not only the amygdala itself but also other structures within the basal ganglia, plays a role in stressful feelings such as irritability, unease, and anxiety. NIDA explained that

> *[these feelings] characterize withdrawal after the drug high fades and thus motivates the person to seek the drug again. This circuit becomes increasingly sensitive with increased drug use. Over time, a person with substance use disorder uses drugs to get temporary relief from this discomfort rather than to get high.*[1]

The prefrontal cortex involves the ability to think, solve problems, plan, make decisions, and exert self-control. The "shifting balance between this circuit and the reward and stress circuits of the basal ganglia and extended amygdala make a person with a substance use disorder seek the drug compulsively with reduced impulse control."[2]

A substance use disorder literally changes the way the brain functions. The longer someone uses a substance, the more the brain changes.

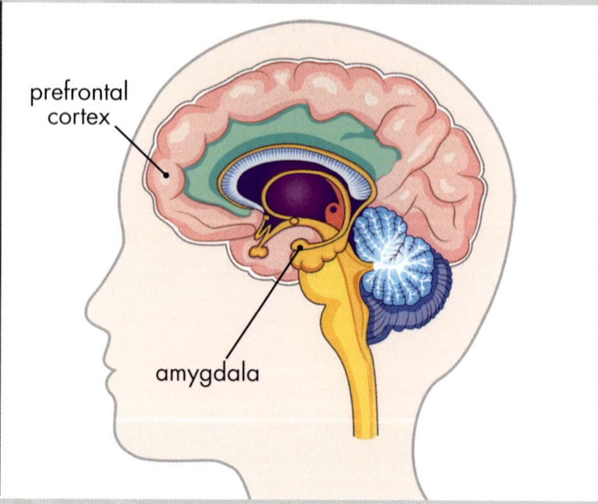

1. "Drugs and the Brain," National Institute on Drug Abuse, last updated July 2018. www.drugabuse.gov/publications/drugs-brains-behavior-science-addiction/drugs-brain.

2. "Drugs and the Brain," National Institute on Drug Abuse.

Cigarettes and cannabis can make someone feel temporarily relaxed, which makes them especially tempting for people who feel stressed. However, an addiction adds to stress over time.

the brain works will change. Its functions will become abnormal. Brain imaging studies performed on people with a long-term substance use disorder show that, in many cases, the brain has actually undergone physical changes. After years of substance abuse, the parts of the brain that control judgment, decision-making, learning, memory, and behavioral control show deterioration.

PREVENTATIVE MEASURES

Early drug use increases the risk of developing a substance use disorder later in life. Therefore, preventing drug use from an early age is essential. The brain is still developing in childhood and the teenage years, so "using drugs at this age has more potential to disrupt brain function in areas critical to motivation, memory, learning, judgment, and behavior control."[21] Teenagers who use drugs tend to have problems with their health, school, family, and friends.

Some people justify using substances by saying they can do whatever they want with their own life, but a substance use disorder affects everyone around the user.

One of the ways drug use can be prevented is through research-based prevention programs. According to NIDA, it is essential for these programs to increase protective factors and reduce or completely remove risk factors. The programs can be used for various age groups in both group and individual settings. NIDA outlined the three types of programs:

- *Universal programs address risk and protective factors common to all children in a given setting, such as a school or community.*
- *Selective programs are for groups of children and teens who have specific factors that put them at increased risk of drug use.*
- *Indicated programs are designed for youth who have already started using drugs.*[22]

While a certain amount of risk-taking is normal throughout adolescence, some of a teen's newfound independence can increase the risk of drug and substance abuse, so researchers are using these programs to try to prevent dangerous behaviors. This is especially important for young adults because the parts of the brain that control decision-making and judgment do not fully develop until a person is in their 20s, which means a teenager may not be able to accurately assess the risks associated with drug use.

SUBSTANCE ABUSE AND TRAUMA

One of the risk factors of developing a drug addiction is trauma, especially childhood trauma such as physical or sexual abuse. Teens who have experienced abuse are three times more likely to turn to substance abuse than those who have not. Experiences in childhood affect the brain's development. As the brain grows and matures throughout different life stages, neural connections are created, strengthened, or discarded depending on the experiences a person has. These neural connections go through what is called synaptic pruning, or the process of strengthening or discarding them. Experiences during childhood can cause synapses to form, strengthen, or break, just like they do as a child learns to walk or talk. Therefore, both positive and negative experiences affect synaptic pruning.

Researchers at the University of Texas studied individuals who had experienced childhood trauma. They reported that

> *being mistreated during childhood caused frequent and extremely high levels of stress that impeded normal brain development. Continuous stress from experiencing frequent maltreatment initiated psychological stress responses that, over time, caused the structural disruptions that were observed in neurological scans and which are likely making victims of childhood trauma vulnerable to substance abuse disorders.*[23]

CELEBRITIES SPEAK UP

Just like average people, celebrities also experience substance use disorders. In fact, celebrities tend to be more likely to have a substance use disorder for various reasons. These include the easy availability of drugs and alcohol at Hollywood parties, having more money to spend on substances, and the pressures of having their private lives opened to the public. Many celebrities have opened up about their experiences, which helps reduce the stigma surrounding these disorders. Tom Holland, Anne Hathaway, John Mulaney, Jason Ritter, Demi Lovato, and countless others have discussed their addictions and their reasons for wanting to overcome them. Some, such as Holland and Hathaway, did not feel good when they were drinking alcohol, realized they had an unhealthy relationship with it, and decided to stop. Both have said they feel better physically and mentally after making this decision. Others, such as Mulaney, had to be told by loved ones how destructive their substance use disorder was to themselves and others.

Lovato has been especially candid about the risk of relapsing. After a relapse in 2018, she said, "What I've learned is that this illness is not something that disappears or fades with time. It is something I must continue to overcome and have not done yet … I look forward to the day where I can say I came out on the other side."[1]

John Mulaney's fifth comedy special, *Baby J*, details some of the humiliating moments his substance use disorder caused.

1. Quoted in Andrew Flanagan, "Demi Lovato: Addiction is 'Not Something That Disappears,'" NPR, August 6, 2018. www.npr.org/2018/08/06/636000566/demi-lovato-addiction-is-not-something-that-disappears.

However, while child abuse can greatly influence a substance use disorder later in life, there are other traumatic and stress-inducing experiences that can do so as well. These include loss of a parent, neglect, and witnessing violence. Because the brain is still developing at such a young age, traumatic experiences from childhood tend to linger, especially when a trusted loved one has been involved in the trauma.

Drugs or alcohol are often used as coping mechanisms to deal with painful memories of abuse, neglect, or the loss of a parent as well as to cope with feelings of isolation and loneliness and deal with problems such as PTSD, depression, or anxiety. When a person with a substance use disorder is receiving treatment for it, mental health issues such as these will also be checked for so the underlying problem can be addressed.

COPING WITH POVERTY

Substance use disorders can affect anyone, but those living in poverty are hit disproportionately hard. These disorders are harder for people living in poverty to beat because resources and treatments typically cost more than they can afford. Research has shown that

> *heroin addiction is more than three times as common in people making less than $20,000 per year compared to those who make $50,000 or more, and higher levels of education are also linked with lower rates of addiction … countries and states with higher levels of inequality tend to have worse mental health and addiction problems than those with less dramatic differences between [the richest] 1% and everyone else.*[24]

When someone is living in poverty, their life is marked by uncertainty—they worry about paying bills, having a home, and putting food on the table. These stressors are generally made worse when someone is out of work. Someone may turn to a substance for temporary relief, become addicted, and then spend even more money on that substance. This makes the stressors that drove them to seek relief worse, reinforcing the addiction in a vicious cycle.

Numerous studies have proven that when there is less income inequality among the citizens of a country, there are lower addiction rates. In an article for the *Guardian*, addiction expert Maia Szalavitz pointed out that

> *decades of survey data … show that the addiction rate among the unemployed is usually around twice as high as among those who have jobs. Some of this unemployment, of course, is addiction-related job loss. But a review of this literature suggests that in many cases, unemployment precedes addiction and that either way, [unemployment] reduces the odds of recovery.*[25]

Research shows that around 90 percent of addictions begin during the teenage and young adult years. Around this time, many people are completing college and starting careers. However, college may not be an option for some people, and whether or not someone has a college degree, it may be hard to find a steady job that pays well. One of the theories as to why addiction hits those who are unemployed harder is that the routines and requirements of a steady job work against substance abuse and addiction behaviors. For example, people are required to be at their job at the designated time and they need to be ready to work—they cannot be hungover or under the influence of drugs. Therefore, without a steady job and with the additional stresses of not having a good income, people may turn to drugs or continue using drugs they had tried previously in order to cope with the circumstances of their lives. This leads many people to argue that the focus should move away from criminalizing drugs and toward fighting inequality and unemployment.

WARNING SIGNS

People may start using drugs for different reasons, but substance use disorders share many common characteristics. A substance use disorder is a disease that impacts every aspect of how a person functions, which means some of the symptoms are highly noticeable. Depending on the type of drug a person is using, some of these can include changes in personality, bloody noses, bloodshot eyes, slurred speech, body tremors, changes in routines and daily activities, changes in hygiene, and unusual financial problems.

Additional signs of a substance use disorder include:

- needing to take more and more of the substance to feel the same effects
- feeling sick or strange when the substance wears off—for example, experiencing headaches, fevers, body tremors, or fatigue
- taking the substance even though it is having a negative impact on one's life
- spending time thinking about how to get more of the substance
- borrowing or stealing money in order to pay for more of the substance

When someone is suffering from a substance use disorder, it is important that they get the help that they need, as it can be impossible to overcome this disorder without the help of professionals.

LIVING WITH SUBSTANCE ABUSE

A person often lives with their substance use disorder for years before seeking help. They often deny they have a problem at all, and they frequently suffer serious health or social consequences, such as liver failure or the loss of their job, before their eyes are opened to the truth. Substance use disorders have a wide range of direct effects on a person's body as well as indirect effects on other aspects of their life. The short- and long-term health effects that a person feels from substance abuse depend on many factors, including how much of the drug has been taken and for how long, what type of drug was taken and in what way, and the person's health before they started taking drugs.

MAKING POOR CHOICES

Indirect effects of a substance use disorder are those that are not directly caused by drugs but by a person's choices surrounding their drug use. When a person has a substance use disorder, they may do things they otherwise would not. For example, they may steal money to acquire more drugs or alcohol because the physical need to use a substance is so strong. Additionally, a person may get into other legal trouble or even go to prison over activities that are related to drug use.

Other indirect effects take a toll on a person's health and safety. For instance, when people share needles—which happens often if they are using a drug that can be injected—they increase their risk of getting diseases such as HIV or hepatitis. A person's sleeping habits, decision-making, and diet may all suffer from drug use, which can cause health problems that are not directly related to the drug, such as malnourishment. Additionally, if someone is going to unknown or dangerous areas to purchase drugs, they may be at risk of violence.

Drug use can also affect employment and schooling. For example, a person with a substance use disorder may drop out of school or lose their job. All of this has an impact on a person's ability to support themselves.

A substance use disorder can cause problems at work and may lead to someone getting fired.

DANGEROUS DRIVING

In 2022, according to the Foundation for Advancing Alcohol Responsibility, drunk driving caused 32 percent of driving fatalities in the United States. This represents an increase from 29 percent in 2017.

In the United States, it is illegal to drive with a blood alcohol concentration (BAC) of .08 or more. BAC is measured by grams of alcohol per deciliter of blood (g/dL). At .08 BAC, muscle coordination becomes poor and speech, vision, balance, hearing, and reaction time are all affected. In addition, it becomes harder to detect danger, and judgment is affected. This makes it harder to drive by impairing a driver's ability to control the speed of the car and process information that is critical to driving, such as how fast the other cars are going and whether a traffic light is about to change color. Even if someone is "buzzed," or has a BAC between .02 and .08, their physical and mental processes are negatively affected.

The effects of drugs on driving depend on how the drug affects the brain. Cannabis slows reaction time, decreases coordination, and impairs a person's judgment of distance and time, so it affects a driver in many of the same ways that alcohol does. Cocaine and meth can cause a driver to be reckless and aggressive. Just because a drug affects the brain in a different way does not mean it is safer to drive under its influence; they are all dangerous in different ways, and it is best for the person who would be driving to stay over at a friend's house or have someone who did not drink or take drugs drive them home safely.

Driving under the influence of any substance is very dangerous. Even if no one is harmed, it can put the driver in serious legal trouble.

One of the most tragic indirect effects of drug use is the impact on the people surrounding a person who has a substance use disorder. A substance use disorder can put a great deal of strain on loved ones, and some of them may find it hard to deal with the stress and trauma of loving someone with a substance use disorder.

PHYSICAL EFFECTS

Substance use disorders have a wide range of physical effects that start even after the first time taking a drug. Short-term effects include things such as an inability to fall asleep as well as changes in appetite, blood pressure, and heart rate. Death is also always a risk with certain drugs.

Substance use disorder affects nearly every organ in the body. The immune system is weakened, which increases the risk of infection or illness. The heart is affected and can start beating abnormally; blood vessels can become infected from injected drugs. The person may also experience abdominal pain, nausea, body temperature changes, and seizures. Additionally, many substances also cause problems in the gastrointestinal system, resulting in damage or decay in the intestines or stomach.

Some drugs or the way they are taken also carry specific risks. For example, injected drugs can cause collapsed veins. Collapsed veins occur because of repeated trauma to an area. Traumas include:

- *Repeated use of the same vein for injection*
- *Use of a blunt needle*
- *Removal of the needle too quickly after injection*
- *Improper injection technique*
- *Drugs that irritate and inflame the veins*[26]

When the same vein is used as an injection site for an extended period of time, the "inside lining of the vein becomes damaged and blood clots develop. If injection continues at the same site, the clots block the vein completely. The sides of the veins heal together and the vein collapses, never to be used again."[27] Symptoms of collapsed veins include cold feet and hands due to loss of circulation, pain at the injection site, and discoloration of the skin in that area. In addition to causing collapsed veins, injecting drugs can also cause skin problems such as collections of pus called abscesses in the area, bruises, bacterial infections, and fungal infections. Another danger of injecting drugs is skin popping. This is when the vein is missed and the needle is injected into muscle or fat instead, resulting in a painful lump.

In addition to open wounds on the skin, one of the characteristics of meth use is what is known as "meth mouth." This describes extreme tooth decay where teeth are broken, discolored, and rotting. Meth mouth happens because the drug has a variety of corrosive chemicals in it. Furthermore, taking meth "causes the salivary glands to dry out, which allows the mouth's acids to eat away at tooth enamel, causing cavities. Teeth are further damaged when users obsessively grind their teeth, binge on sugary food and drinks, and neglect to brush or floss for long periods of time."[28] The amount of damage meth causes in the mouth cannot be reversed, even among short-term users of the drug.

MENTAL EFFECTS

When a person takes a substance, they experience more than just physical effects such as changes in sight or sensation. According to NIDA, "Chronic use of some drugs can lead to both short- and long-term changes in the brain, which can lead to mental health issues including paranoia, depression, anxiety, aggression, hallucinations, and other problems."[29]

A temporary change in mood is expected—and generally desired—when someone uses a substance. People may use cannabis to feel more relaxed, alcohol to feel more outgoing, or ecstasy to feel happier. However, if someone develops a dependency or a substance use disorder, their brain stops being able to release the right amount of neurotransmitters on its own to create those feelings without the use of drugs.

A CULTURE SHIFT

Gen Z, which refers to people born between 1997 and 2012, and Gen Alpha, which refers to people born between 2013 and 2025, have shown a much lower interest in drinking alcohol than previous generations. In fact, 67 percent of young people in 2024 reported never having tried alcohol.

Experts say there are likely multiple reasons for this shift. One might be the legalization and wider availability of cannabis, which young people may choose to consume instead of alcohol. Another might be the success of persistent messaging about alcohol's negative health effects. A third might be the increase in online socialization and the decrease in in-person socialization. Alcohol is typically consumed in higher amounts at parties rather than when someone is alone in their house.

This changing attitude toward alcohol has forced bars to adapt in order to remain profitable. Many bars now offer mocktails, or cocktails made without alcohol. Some "sober bars" offer non-alcoholic drinks exclusively. Nonalcoholic beers and mixed drinks are becoming much more popular as well.

When this happens, the person starts needing the drug all the time to feel "normal." If they are unable to take it, they may feel irritable, anxious, or depressed.

These effects are heightened when someone already has a mental illness. Someone who has clinical depression—a mental illness that involves feelings of hopelessness, despair, and worthlessness—may drink because they feel better when they are drunk.

A LIFESAVING DRUG

An overdose is one of the most infamous effects of addiction, and overdoses have been in the news more and more as the opioid crisis has worsened. During an opioid overdose, the central nervous system and respiratory system slow down, or depress. Naloxone, also called Evzio or Narcan, rapidly counters this life-threatening state and allows the person experiencing the overdose to breathe normally. It works by binding to the opioid receptors in the brain and blocking the effects of other opioids, thus restoring normal respiration. Naloxone only works if it is given to someone who has opioids in their system at the time, so it is not meant to be taken in advance to prevent an overdose. It is non-addictive and can be administered by anyone.

Naloxone can be administered in a number of ways, including injection or being sprayed into the nostrils. Naloxone that is sprayed has a higher concentration than it does when injected. It wears off in about 20 to 90 minutes, but the person who was given naloxone should be observed until medical personnel arrive and for two hours after that by the medical personnel themselves to make sure respiration is normal.

Naloxone, or Narcan, can save the life of a person who has overdosed on opioids.

However, this causes even more problems. Firstly, someone cannot be drunk all the time without causing serious problems to their physical health as well as to their daily life; for instance, if they go to work drunk, they are likely to be fired. Secondly, as alcohol changes their brain chemistry, they might feel even more depressed after they sober up than they previously did. This often makes it harder to give up drinking because they do not want to sober up. Some drugs can also interfere with prescribed medication that a person takes to keep the symptoms of their mental illness under control.

Some people do not have a mental illness but do have a genetic predisposition for one. Most mental illnesses are at least partially genetic, which means certain genes that play a role in those illnesses are passed down from parent to child. Someone who has several family members with a certain mental illness likely also has genes connected to that illness themselves. However, this is not a guarantee that someone will develop a mental illness. The second factor in most mental illnesses is environmental: Something the person encounters—including extreme stress, a head injury, or drug use—may "turn on" mental illness genes. Studies have found that, in particular, long-term ecstasy use is associated with the development of depression and long-term cannabis use is associated with the development of schizophrenia in people who have a genetic predisposition to such illnesses.

According to Drugs.ie, an informational website maintained by Ireland's official health services department, "It is possible that if you have a pre-existing risk which you may not be aware of, there is a higher chance that using cannabis will trigger an episode of schizophrenia. These risks are also greater in younger people who use cannabis and those that smoke it more regularly."[30]

OVERDOSE

Having too much of a substance in the body at one time can be extremely harmful to the user's health. Alcohol poisoning occurs when a person has had a large amount of alcohol over a short period of time. When this happens, breathing, heart rate, gag reflex, and body temperature are all affected. Symptoms of alcohol poisoning include seizures, vomiting, confusion, slowed breathing (less than 8 breaths per minute), pale or blue-tinged skin, low body temperature, irregular breathing (more than 10 seconds in between breaths), and becoming unresponsive (falling unconscious and not responding to attempts to wake them up). If a person is showing even a few of these symptoms, they should be taken to a doctor immediately. The longer someone waits, the higher the person's risk of becoming unresponsive and dying.

People who drink too much alcohol at one time may black out (continue functioning without remembering what they did) or pass out. This can also happen if they mix alcohol and other drugs.

Some drug overdoses are intentional as an act of suicide, but many are accidental. Certain situations, such as a relapse, put a person at greater risk of overdosing. When someone is seeking treatment for an addiction and they have gone without the drug in their system for a while and then use it again, they may use the same amount they were used to having before. However, their body no longer has a tolerance for that amount, and an overdose occurs.

A person who is on the verge of overdosing is rarely aware of the danger they are in. However, other people surrounding them may notice signs such as cold hands, vomiting, drowsiness, and slowed breathing.

Getting someone medical help for an overdose is crucial, especially in the case of opioids and alcohol because these can quickly cause death. Even if a person survives their overdose, though, their body or brain can suffer permanent damage that leaves them disabled for life. For this reason, experts caution that keeping careful track of how much of a substance has been consumed is the best course of action when someone is unable to avoid consuming the substance at all.

TREATMENT OPTIONS

Seeking treatment is the first step to recovering from a substance use disorder. However, many people never take this step, even when they know the substance is doing a lot of damage to their body and quality of life. One reason for this is the fear that they will be shamed or abandoned for admitting that they have a substance use disorder. Someone who is suffering with this disorder needs support not only from their loved ones, but also from trained medical professionals. These experts can help them with the withdrawal symptoms and provide them with therapies that also deal with any underlying issues that may have prompted their substance use.

REDUCING HARM

One approach to treating substance use disorders is harm reduction. This is a set of strategies that is aimed at reducing the negative consequences of drug use. There is no specific formula for putting these strategies in place because the idea behind harm reduction is to demand interventions that reflect specific needs of the individual and community. While there is no specific harm reduction formula, there are certain principles people aim to follow.

First, harm reduction accepts that drug use is part of the world. Instead of ignoring drug use or condemning it, harm reduction instead works to

RACIAL STEREOTYPES

In 2018, the movie *Beautiful Boy*, starring Steve Carell and Timothée Chalamet, was released. Based on a true story, the movie follows David Sheff (Carell) and his son, Nic (Chalamet), as David works to get Nic help for his use of multiple drugs, including cannabis, alcohol, cocaine, ecstasy, heroin, and crystal meth.

The movie received mixed reviews. Some people were moved by the film's emotional portrayal of how addiction affects not only the person who is using drugs, but their loved ones as well. The movie was also praised for showing how easily someone can relapse, how much hard work recovery takes, and how much recovery can depend on the support someone receives from their friends and family.

However, some people criticized *Beautiful Boy* for not acknowledging the different ways addiction affects white people and people of color. While the movie is based on a true story about a white family, Joshua Rivera wrote in an article for *GQ* magazine that the movie focused too narrowly on stereotypes: "It's got two scenes where white people buy drugs from brown people. And it seems *wholly* uninterested in examining a reality wherein, were the film's David Sheff not a nice white journalist of some means, the kind of help he'd get might be totally different—if nonexistent."[1]

Many studies have shown the existence of racial bias in the way people who abuse drugs are viewed; white people are more frequently seen as victims of drug pushers or of addiction itself, while people of color are more often portrayed as criminals who take drugs because they enjoy getting high or as people who make a selfish choice to continue using drugs even though it hurts their loved ones. In real life, this type of bias can cause medical professionals to refuse to help people of color with their addictions if they are seen as less "deserving" of help than white people. Furthermore, as people of color are often disproportionately poorer than white people, they are less likely to have money available to check into a rehabilitation center.

1. Joshua Rivera, "The White Innocence of Beautiful Boy," *GQ*, October 15, 2018. www.gq.com/story/the-white-innocence-of-beautiful-boy.

minimize its effects. The philosophy also recognizes that drug use is complex and that the severity of drug use varies. Some people may use certain drugs only a few times, while others use them multiple times each day. Harm reduction also acknowledges that some ways of using drugs are more dangerous than others.

The harm reduction philosophy also follows these principles:

- *Establishes quality of individual and community life and well-being—not necessarily cessation [stopping] of all drug use—as the criteria for successful interventions and policies.*
- *Calls for the non-judgmental, non-coercive provision of services and resources to people who use drugs and the communities in which they live in order to assist them in reducing attendant harm.*
- *Ensures that drug users and those with a history of drug use routinely have a real*

Some people dislike the idea of naloxone being publicly available, believing that it encourages drug use. Others say that not having the kit available will not discourage use and will increase a user's risk of suffering a fatal overdose.

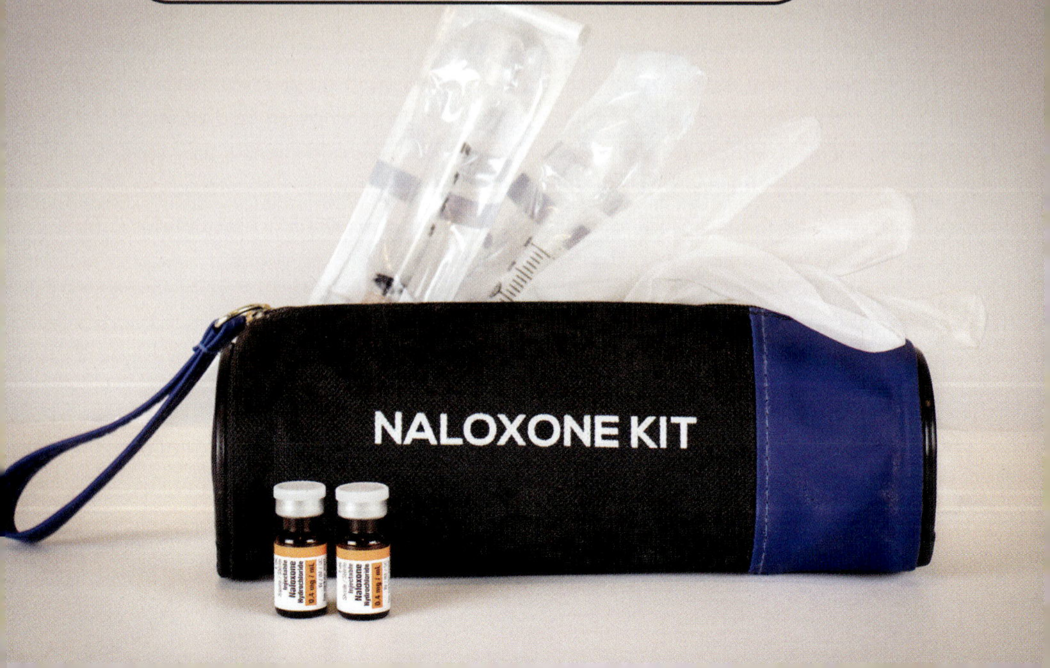

voice in the creation of programs and policies designed to serve them.

- *Affirms drug users themselves as the primary agents of reducing the harms of their drug use, and seeks to empower users to share information and support each other in strategies which meet their actual conditions of use.*
- *Recognizes that the realities of poverty, class, racism, social isolation, past trauma, sex-based discrimination and other social inequalities affect both people's vulnerability to and capacity for effectively dealing with drug-related harm.*[31]

Most importantly, harm reduction does not ignore the fact that there is real, tragic harm associated with drug use.

DSM-5 CRITERIA

A thorough evaluation is required before someone can be diagnosed with a substance use disorder. These evaluations often include an alcohol or drug counselor, psychiatrist, psychologist, and a series of lab tests. To diagnose a substance use disorder, mental health professionals turn to the American Psychological Association's *Diagnostic and Statistical Manual of Mental Disorders, Fifth Edition* (*DSM-5*). This manual is the guidebook for diagnosing different disorders.

The *DSM-5* recognizes disorders resulting from 10 classes of drugs, including hallucinogens, alcohol, inhalants, opioids, cannabis, caffeine, tobacco, stimulants, and other or unknown substances. The *DSM-5* also recognizes that not everyone is equally predisposed to a substance use disorder—some people are more likely than others to develop an addiction.

A doctor can diagnose someone with a substance use disorder. However, most general practitioners are not trained in treating the disorder and will refer the patient to a specialist.

The *DSM-5* specifies the criteria to diagnose a substance use disorder and determine its severity. The criteria for a substance use disorder, according to the *DSM-5*, are:

1. *Taking the substance in larger amounts or for longer than you're meant to.*
2. *Wanting to cut down or stop using the substance but not managing to.*
3. *Spending a lot of time getting, using, or recovering from use of the substance.*
4. *Cravings and urges to use the substance.*
5. *Not managing to do what you should at work, home, or school because of substance use.*
6. *Continuing to use, even when it causes problems in relationships.*
7. *Giving up important social, occupational, or recreational activities because of substance use.*
8. *Using substances again and again, even when it puts you in danger.*
9. *Continuing to use, even when you know you have a physical or psychological problem that could have been caused or made worse by the substance.*
10. *Needing more of the substance to get the effect you want (tolerance).*
11. *Development of withdrawal symptoms, which can be relieved by taking more of the substance.*[32]

The severity of a substance use disorder depends on how many of the criteria the patient meets.

Two to three of the symptoms listed in the criteria equal a mild substance use disorder, four to five symptoms equal a moderate substance use disorder, and six or more equal a severe substance use disorder.

SYMPTOMS OF WITHDRAWAL

There is no cure for substance use disorders. There is also not a one-size-fits-all approach to treatment because everyone is different. Not only does the same drug sometimes affect two different people in very different ways, people also tend to mix drugs together, and there are many possible combinations that have to be addressed in different ways. For example, one person might frequently take cocaine and heroin, while another might take cocaine and ecstasy. These two people will have very different reactions to cocaine because of the presence of the other drug in their system.

Treating a substance use disorder is a complex process. Some aspects of treatment address the drug use itself, while others focus on the person's role in the community and their family. The disorder is treated in specialized treatment facilities, doctors' offices, and mental health facilities. Depending on how severe it is, patients might benefit from either inpatient or outpatient settings. Inpatient means they check into a rehabilitation clinic, often called "rehab." Outpatient means they continue to live their life as normal but see a therapist or other specialist regularly.

Most treatment programs begin by clearing the person's body of drugs in a medically managed withdrawal and detoxification—commonly called detoxing—process. Detoxing from a drug involves completely clearing the body of drugs to stop the physiological effects they have. It can involve gradually decreasing the drug until the person is off of it or replacing the drug with a different substance, such as methadone for opioid addictions. This is done to minimize the withdrawal symptoms that occur when the body no longer has access to a drug it is physically dependent on. In some cases, someone can quit a drug "cold turkey," or all at once, but with some drugs, doing this results in withdrawal symptoms so severe that they can cause further harm to the person's body. Withdrawal symptoms can include flu-like symptoms, seizures, tremors, restlessness, and depression or anxiety.

Detox and withdrawal are just the start of the recovery process, though. A person cannot simply detox and be done with their addiction.

This picture was taken at an Overdose Awareness March. Knowing about a problem is the first step toward fixing it.

ADDRESSING OVERPRESCRIPTION

As the extent of the opioid crisis gradually became clear over several years, people began to be concerned about the overprescription of these drugs. Some organizations have started advocating for a decrease in the number of opioid prescriptions and have encouraged the medical community to look into alternative pain management therapies, especially when the pain is not severe. Between 2011 and 2020, there was a 44.4 percent decrease in the amount of opioid prescriptions across all 50 U.S. states, which shows that doctors are becoming wary of prescribing a medication that has been proven to have a high risk of addiction.

Many experts have noted that simply banning opioids is not a good option, since no more than 29 percent of patients misuse their opioids and no more than 12 percent become addicted. While these numbers are still far too high, they show that the majority of patients use their opioids responsibly, and for some people, they are the only thing that treats their severe, chronic pain. Patrice Harris, chair of the American Medical Association Opioid Task Force, said, "We need well-designed initiatives that bring together public and private insurers, policymakers, public health infrastructure and communities with the shared goal to improve access and coverage for comprehensive pain management and treatment for substance abuse disorders."[1]

In a study published in August 2018, researchers set out to answer the question of whether doctors would exhibit more care in prescribing opioid medications if they were made aware of the risks of opioids firsthand. One of the findings of the study was that many doctors do not learn of a patient's death from an opioid overdose—the patient simply disappears from their practice. Between July 2015 and June 2016, a randomized trial was performed on 861 clinicians. These clinicians had prescribed opioids to 170 patients who had died from an overdose of opioid medications. Half of the clinicians would receive a letter that a patient died of an overdose. The letter stated that the patient had died and provided information from the CDC about safe opioid prescribing guidelines. Within three months after receiving this letter, the doctors in this group decreased their opioid prescriptions by 9.7 percent. In addition, doctors who received letters were 7 percent less likely to use opioids for a first-time patient and also less likely to start with a high dose.

1. "Study Finds 22 Percent Decrease in Opioid Prescriptions," AAFP, April 25, 2018. www.aafp.org/news/health-of-the-public/20180425opioidstudy.html.

INPATIENT AND OUTPATIENT CARE

Inpatient treatment can be either long-term or short-term. Long-term provides care 24 hours a day, 7 days a week in a non-hospital setting. It is also known as residential treatment because of the comfortable, home-like environment. The therapeutic community (TC) model is the best-known residential treatment model, and length of stay is generally between six and twelve months. This type of treatment model involves resocialization and uses the center's community as components of treatment. Treatment in this type of facility is highly structured. The patient is forced to examine their beliefs, destructive patterns of behavior, and self-concepts. These destructive beliefs are then replaced with more constructive and harmonious beliefs and ways of interacting with others.

Short-term inpatient treatment is generally used to treat an alcohol addiction. The brief yet intensive program consists of a stay of three to six weeks in a treatment facility, followed by outpatient therapy and meetings in groups such as Alcoholics Anonymous (AA). It is important that the person continues going to meetings and outpatient programs after their inpatient treatment is done so they are able to reduce the risk of relapse.

Outpatient treatment costs less than inpatient treatment, and the intensity of the program varies. This type of treatment is suitable for people with an extensive support system. However, if the program is low intensity, then it is not much more than education about drugs. Therefore, intensive day treatment programs are recommended in this situation because they are comparable to inpatient programs. Group counseling is often a major component of this type of program.

Group therapy can help people with a substance use disorder connect with others who understand what they are going through.

In addition to treating the substance use disorder itself, treatment programs examine the possibility of underlying mental health problems such as depression, anxiety, or PTSD. This is because these problems are often what drive people to use substances in the first place. If they are not addressed, the risk of relapse is very high.

ADDRESSING THE PROBLEM

Substance use disorder is not just a private matter. It is a public health problem with numerous effects on society, loved ones, and the user's life. Considering how large of an impact a substance use disorder has on every aspect of a person's life, nearly everyone agrees that the problem needs to be addressed, but many people have different ideas regarding the best way to do that. One idea is to have people who have lost a loved one to drug use or who have recovered from their own addiction travel to schools to talk about the dangers of substance abuse. Others focus on researching the lasting effects of drug use or finding the best way to prevent drug use in the first place. Still others continue to focus on legislation and criminalization of drugs—a controversial area, since many argue that criminalization has already been proven not to work.

DRUG ABUSE AFFECTS EVERYONE

According to the CDC, "Public health is the science of protecting and improving the health of people and their communities. This work is achieved by promoting healthy lifestyles, researching disease and injury prevention, and directing, preventing and responding to infectious diseases."[33] Public health is concerned with an overall population—it can be a small community of 1,000 people, an entire country, or a region of the world.

The CDC has identified 10 main concerns of public health. These include food safety, health care-associated infections, HIV, heart disease and stroke, alcohol-related harms, nutrition and obesity, tobacco use, teen pregnancy, prescription drug overdose, and motor vehicle injuries. Substance use disorders overlap many of these problems.

Many experts believe it is important that substance use disorders are treated as public health problems instead of criminal justice problems. This way, the focus is placed on the health of the community or individual. Treating substance use disorders as a criminal justice problem has not helped in the past because it does not focus on the health of the person or treatment of the person's addiction. Since addiction causes people to keep using a substance regardless of the negative impacts it has on their life, the threat of going to prison for using illegal drugs is not enough to get them to stop; it only punishes them for something they cannot physically control.

Going to prison also does not cure a substance use disorder. According to Columbia University, 65 percent of people in prison have a substance use disorder, but only 11 percent of them receive any sort of treatment. Focusing on substance use disorders as a criminal justice issue only places more people in prisons that may already be overcrowded, and it increases the chances of recidivism, or returning to crime after getting out of prison. One study found that recidivism rates for people with a substance use disorder dropped by 50 percent when those people received treatment in prison for their disorder.

LEGAL REGULATIONS

In 2017, President Donald Trump declared that the opioid epidemic had become a public health emergency. In October 2018, he signed a legislative package that he believed would help end drug addiction. The bill is known as the SUPPORT for Patients and Communities Act, and it directs funding toward different avenues to end drug addiction, including increasing access to treatment for substance use disorders. Congress reauthorized the act in 2023, giving it funding for another five years.

This legislative package includes 70 bills, some of which offer incentives to the National Institutes of Health (NIH) to make finding non-addictive painkillers a priority. The Synthetics Trafficking and Overdose Prevention Act, or STOP Act, was included in the package. As NBC News explained:

> *[This act] establishes parameters to crack down on shipments of fentanyl, a synthetic opioid, from entering the U.S. Currently, the U.S. Postal Service is the only transportation carrier that does not collect electronic information on overseas cargo, which makes it harder for Customs and Border Protection agents to screen packages for drugs.*[34]

With this law, Trump was focusing on the fact that most fentanyl comes from China via the U.S. Postal Service. Not all fentanyl arrives in the United States this way, though. There are multiple pipelines for getting fentanyl into the United States. Some go from China to Canada to the United States; Canada is under less suspicion than China, so shipments that come to the United States that way are less likely to be flagged by border patrol agents than

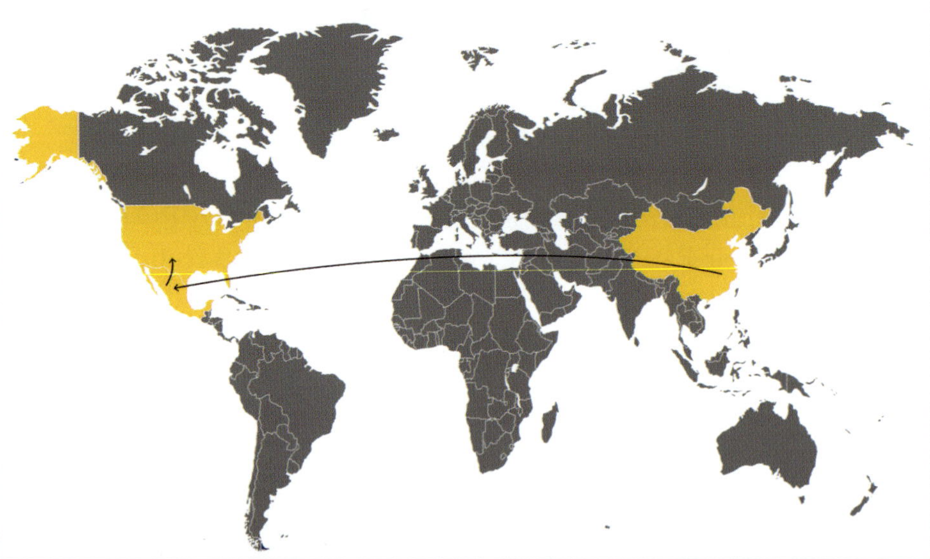

This map shows one common route fentanyl takes, from China to Mexico to the United States.

ones that arrive at an airport from China. Some fentanyl or the chemicals to make it are shipped to Mexico, where they are turned into a finished product and smuggled into the United States, generally via San Diego, California.

A PERFORMATIVE ACT?

While some people have applauded these measures, others have argued not enough is being done, especially considering other measures that the Trump administrations have taken in regard to cutting funding for health-care programs such as Medicaid. Medicaid provides health coverage for low-income citizens, and some of these people may be suffering from a substance use disorder. Democrat Frank Pallone, a Congressman representing New Jersey, stated:

President Trump and Congressional Republicans continue to threaten to undermine the health care that Americans rely on for opioid treatment … It is disingenuous [misleading] at best to promise relief to people struggling with opioid addiction while also attempting to cut funding for Medicaid and eliminate protections for people with pre-existing conditions, which include opioid use disorder.[35]

Experts on public health agree with the parts of the SUPPORT Act that increase access to treatment. These experts believe this is an important part of stopping the opioid epidemic. The SUPPORT Act removed "an old provision that did not allow those with substance abuse issues to access mental health facilities with more than 16 beds for treatment under Medicaid. The bill also creates a grant

The U.S. government has passed laws to try to address the opioid epidemic. However, there is some debate over the effectiveness of these laws.

HIT HARDER

The opioid epidemic has affected people all over the United States, but some states have been hit harder than others. For example, a Fair Health study that analyzed 26 billion insurance claims from 2002 to 2017 found that Florida, West Virginia, Rhode Island, Kentucky, and California suffered the most from the opioid epidemic during that period.

One of the study's discoveries was that treatment for pain varied among the states. If pain is not appropriately addressed by a medical professional or if the person is building a tolerance to the prescribed opioid, they may try a harder and more aggressive drug, such as heroin. Mental health counseling was also shown to make a significant difference. New York was the only state offering group counseling as one of the five most common procedures for opioid use disorder, and only five states—Delaware, Nebraska, North Dakota, South Dakota, and Wisconsin—included 45 minutes of psychotherapy as one of the five most common procedures. These states had some of the lowest rates of opioid addiction in the country.

Another factor in the rise of opioid abuse in some states is that there may be competition between doctors in a certain area to get and keep patients. Therefore, in an effort to attract patients, some doctors may be more likely to prescribe opioids than others. While people should listen to their doctors, they should also be comfortable asking questions and speaking up when they are uncomfortable with something. Helping patients learn how to advocate for themselves and tell doctors that they do not want to take opioids may further decrease the number of prescriptions in the United States.

program for states to help recovery centers and addiction specialists increase their quality of care."[36]

However, people such as Keith Humphreys, a professor at Stanford University who helped the Senate and House staff craft this piece of legislation, believe the bill does not do enough to address deeper issues relating to drug addiction and diseases such as HIV/AIDS that can result from things such as sharing needles.

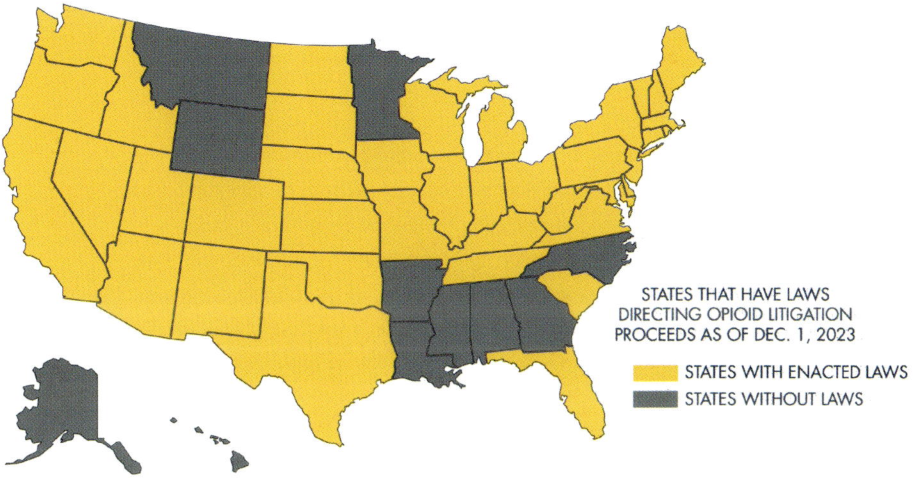

Many state and local governments have sued opioid makers for the harm their product has done. The states shown in yellow have passed laws that require the money from these lawsuits, or litigation, to be used to fund public health programs that help treat or prevent substance use disorders, according to Temple University.

ONGOING RESEARCH

Researchers are continuing to study addiction and how to best treat it. Mike Saladin, a researcher and clinical psychologist with the Medical University of South Carolina in Charleston, believes that addiction is tied to memory and learning. In a study performed in 2018, researchers with the university observed the effects of memory on people who were addicted to cocaine. To trigger their craving for the drug, one participant watched a video of people using cocaine and was also shown drug

AN INEFFECTIVE DETERRENT

Public restrooms are common sites for illicit activities such as drug use. This is because they can be easily accessed, are isolated, and do not have surveillance cameras. To counter this, one of the measures some businesses are taking is to install blue lights in the bathrooms. The blue lights make it harder for heroin users to inject the drug into their veins because it is not easy to see veins under the colored light.

Drug use in bathrooms is a concern among business owners because of "the safety of their customers but also of their employees—the ones cleaning up blood splatter, picking up used needles or calling 911 when a user has overdosed in the washroom."[1] However, these blue lights are causing additional concerns. The *Harm Reduction Journal* warned that people will still try to inject drugs even with the blue lights, which increases the risk of an injection injury. People who have recovered from a drug addiction agree with this, pointing out that someone could just use the flashlight on their cell phone. However, even if a person does not have a flashlight, they are likely to still try to use drugs. Some people who were surveyed even stated that they had previously used drugs in a room with blue lights and would do it again even though there were many risks and consequences.

Some security experts have advised businesses that the blue lights could help to a degree, but additional measures need to be added, such as having employees monitor the restrooms frequently. Some recommend not using the lights at all.

1. Lindsey Bever, "A Plan to Keep Drug Users from Shooting Up in Public Restrooms—and Why It May Be a Bad Idea," Washington Post, June 29, 2018. www.washingtonpost.com/news/to-your-health/wp/2018/06/29/the-plan-to-keep-drug-users-from-shooting-up-in-public-restrooms-and-why-it-may-be-abad-idea/?utm_term=.864de7b395b2.

paraphernalia as well as a bag of what looked like powder or crack cocaine. The person was then given a dose of propranolol, which interferes with the memory-forming abilities of the brain. Following the propranolol treatment, patients were monitored on-site at the test facility and then carefully monitored outside of the facility for six weeks.

The goal of this study was to reactivate memories of using drugs and then weaken those memories with the propranolol. The theory was that as the memories lost power, the drug cravings would also decrease. Throughout the 2010s, there have

Some places have tried using blue light in bathrooms to discourage intravenous drug use. However, people with a substance use disorder are highly likely to take risks when it comes to using their drug of choice.

been more than 10 other lab experiments done on the link between memory and drug use, often on rodents.

In 2023, a large group of scientists announced that they had created two new medications that might help with addiction and depression. These medications come from a material called ibogaine, which is found in the roots of a central African plant called the iboga. Taking ibogaine on its own causes many negative health effects, such as an abnormal heartbeat. Scientists isolated the molecules in ibogaine that help with addiction and used only those to create the new medicines, allowing them to be effective without having bad side effects.

Limited trials in mice and people with opioid addictions have shown that ibogaine is very effective at treating addiction. Because it targets depression as well, it helps treat a major underlying cause of addiction. Furthermore, it appears to lessen withdrawal symptoms, which are a major cause of relapse. Several people who had unsuccessfully tried other addiction treatments in the past credited ibogaine with helping them finally break free.

LOOKING TO OTHER COUNTRIES

Drug addiction is not a problem that only the United States faces, but some other countries look at drug addiction differently by removing the stigma surrounding it and helping the people who suffer from an addiction instead of treating them like criminals. One of the most important things that other countries, such as Portugal, do is to treat addiction as a disease. The way they view the situation is that, just as they would not arrest someone for having diabetes, depression, or some other illness, they would not arrest someone for having a drug addiction. By treating drug addiction as a medical issue, other countries have made great strides in decreasing their addiction rates.

In the 1990s, nearly 1 percent of Portugal's citizens had a heroin use disorder, and it had become the primary public health problem of the country. This also contributed to the fact that Portugal had the highest rate of HIV infection in the European Union. By 1998, a task force had been created that consisted of social and mental health care workers, judges, and doctors. They came up with a new program that few anticipated: They completely decriminalized drugs in 2001. People who had personal supplies of drugs would not be arrested or put in prison. Instead, they were offered therapy. Imprisoning people costs more than treating them for drug addictions, so the task force made the argument that treating people would save money.

The new decriminalization policy stated that if someone had less than a 10-day supply of a drug—indicating that someone was using the drug themselves rather than selling it to other people—instead of being sent to prison, they would be sent to a local commission made up of a doctor, lawyer, and social worker. There, they would learn about the treatments available to them. Portugal also created outreach teams that go to places where people are known to take drugs and offer clean, new needles as well as

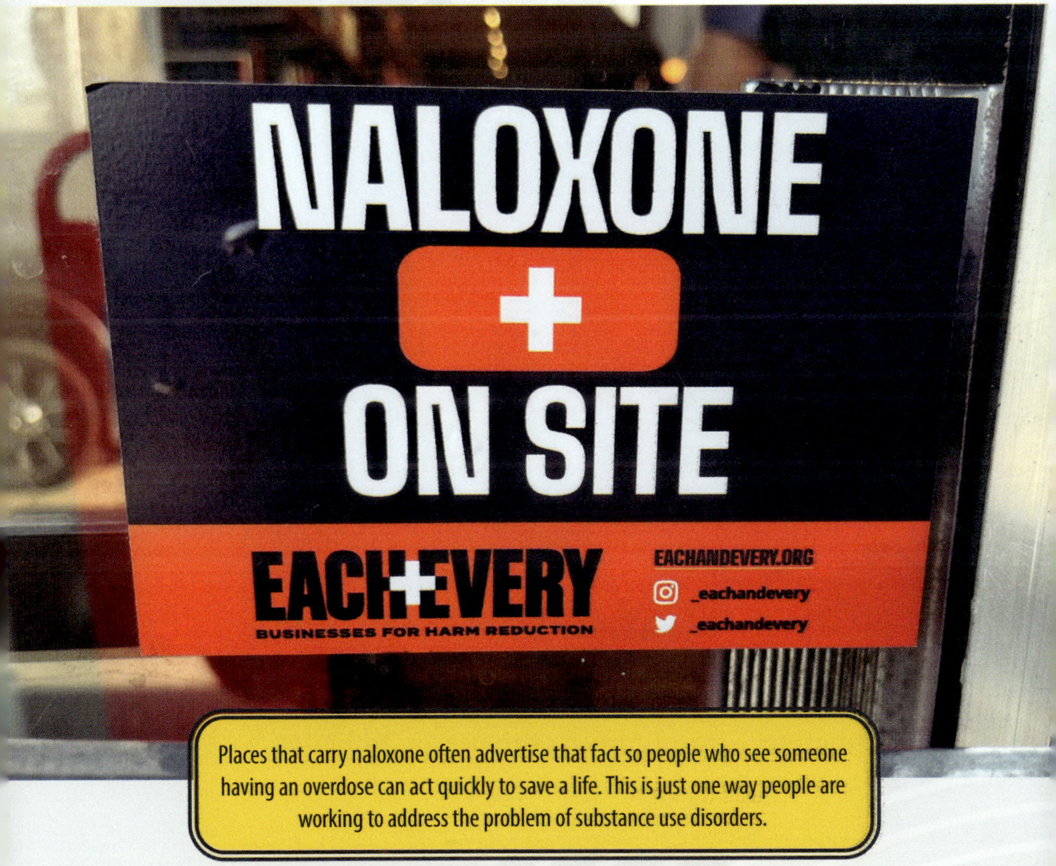

Places that carry naloxone often advertise that fact so people who see someone having an overdose can act quickly to save a life. This is just one way people are working to address the problem of substance use disorders.

psychological support. Additionally, Portugal proposed opening supervised drug consumption facilities, where people can take drugs in safe conditions under the supervision of trained medical experts. Many other European countries, including France, Germany, Spain, and Greece, have opened these since 1986, and evidence has shown that they reduce the rates of HIV and hepatitis C transmission. They also keep people with a substance use disorder off the streets, where they might cause a commotion or scare people when they are high and not in control of their actions. Several U.S. cities have considered opening them as well, but many American citizens are opposed to them because in the United States, there is still a very strong stigma around drug use.

By 2009, Portugal's program showed positive results. The rate of new HIV infections that were spread through the sharing of needles had dropped, teenagers' use of illegal drugs had dropped, and the amount of people seeking treatment for drug use more than doubled.

Some people are looking to Portugal's approach for inspiration as to what the United States should do. Although they are different countries and the exact same approach might not work, there is still a lesson to be learned from Portugal's experiment: The best way to address substance use disorders is to treat them as a medical problem rather than a criminal problem.

Substance use disorders will always be a threat as long as people continue to use addictive substances. There are ways to help reduce and treat this disorder, but the best way to avoid the mental, emotional, and physical problems that come with an addiction is to minimize the use of addictive substances or simply avoid them altogether.

NOTES

INTRODUCTION: A MISUNDERSTOOD DISEASE

1. "Understanding Drug Use and Addiction," National Institute on Drug Abuse, last updated June 2018. www.drugabuse.gov/publications/drugfacts/understanding-drug-use-addiction.

2. "Understanding Drug Use and Addiction," National Institute on Drug Abuse.

CHAPTER ONE: ADDICTIVE SUBSTANCES

3. Quoted in Jane O'Brien, "The Time When Americans Drank All Day Long," BBC News, March 9, 2015. www.bbc.com/news/magazine-31741615.

4. Andrew Curry, "Our 9,000-Year Love Affair with Booze," *National Geographic*, February 2017. www.nationalgeographic.com/magazine/2017/02/alcohol-discovery-addiction-booze-human-culture/.

5. "The Different Types of Alcohol—A Bartender's Guide," Crafty Bartending, accessed on August 28, 2018. www.craftybartending.com/types-of-alcohol/.

6. "Alcohol," NIDA for Teens, last updated January 2016. teens.drugabuse.gov/drug-facts/alcohol.

7. Alina Bradford, "What Is THC?," Live Science, May 18, 2017. www.livescience.com/24553-what-is-thc.html.

8. "Is Cannabis Addictive?," National Institute on Drug Abuse, last updated June 2018. www.drugabuse.gov/publications/research-reports/cannabis/cannabis-addictive.

9. Quoted in Annie Lowrey, "America's Invisible Pot Addicts," *The Atlantic*, August 20, 2018. www.theatlantic.com/ideas/archive/2018/08/americas-invisible-pot-addicts/567886/.

10. German Lopez, "Cannabis Is Legal for Medical Purposes in 32 States," Vox, last updated November 14, 2018. www.vox.com/identities/2018/8/20/17938366/medical-cannabis-legalization-states-map.

11. "Drug Scheduling," DEA.gov, accessed on December 1, 2018. www.dea.gov/drug-scheduling.

12. Lopez, "Cannabis Is Legal for Medical Purposes in 32 States."

13. "Transforming Opium Poppies into Heroin," PBS *Frontline*, accessed on October 25, 2018. www.pbs.org/wgbh/pages/frontline/shows/heroin/transform/.

14. "Transforming Opium Poppies into Heroin," PBS *Frontline*.

15. Smitha Bhandari, ed., "Heroin: What You Need to Know," WebMD,

May 20, 2018. www.webmd.com/mental-health/addiction/heroin-use.

16. Jen Christensen, "How Heroin Kills You," CNN, August 29, 2014. www.cnn.com/2014/02/04/health/how-heroin-kills/.

17. Healthwise Staff, "Repair of Nasal Septal Perforation," PeaceHealth, March 27, 2018. www.peacehealth.org/medical-topics/id/tu6493.

18. Jason S. Hamilton, "Septal Perforation Brief Facts," Osborne Head & Neck Institute Division of Plastic Surgery, accessed on November 2, 2018. www.perforatedseptum.com/perforated-septum-treatment/.

19. "What are the Short-Term Effects of Cocaine Use?," National Institute on Drug Abuse, last updated May 2016. www.drugabuse.gov/publications/research-reports/cocaine/what-are-short-term-effects-cocaine-use.

CHAPTER TWO: A DEEPER UNDERSTANDING

20. "Understanding Drug Use and Addiction," National Institute on Drug Abuse.

21. "Preventing Drug Misuse and Addiction: The Best Strategy," National Institute on Drug Abuse, last updated July 2018. www.drugabuse.gov/publications/drugs-brains-behavior-science-addiction/preventing-drug-misuse-addiction-best-strategy.

22. "Preventing Drug Misuse and Addiction," National Institute on Drug Abuse.

23. Dane O'Leary, "The Unfortunate Connection Between Childhood Trauma and Addiction in Adulthood," Foundations Recovery Network, accessed on February 6, 2019. www.dualdiagnosis.org/unfortunate-connection-childhood-trauma-addiction-adulthood/.

24. Maia Szalavitz, "Addictions Are Harder to Kick When You're Poor. Here's Why," *Guardian*, June 1, 2016. www.theguardian.com/commentisfree/2016/jun/01/drug-addiction-income-inequality-impacts-recovery.

25. Szalavitz, "Addictions Are Harder to Kick When You're Poor."

CHAPTER THREE: LIVING WITH SUBSTANCE ABUSE

26. "Collapsed Veins Due to IV Drug Use," Rehabs.com, accessed on February 7, 2019. luxury.rehabs.com/iv-drug-use/collapsed-veins/.

27. "Collapsed Veins Due to IV Drug Use," Rehabs.com.

28. "How Meth Destroys the Body," PBS *Frontline*, last updated May 17, 2011. www.pbs.org/wgbh/pages/frontline/meth/body/.

29. "Mental Health Effects," National Institute on Drug Abuse, last updated March 2017. www.drugabuse.gov/

publications/health-consequences-drug-misuse/mental-health-effects.

30. "Drugs and Mental Health," Drugs.ie, accessed on March 6, 2019. www.drugs.ie/drugs_info/about_drugs/mental_health/.

CHAPTER FOUR: TREATMENT OPTIONS

31. "Principles of Harm Reduction," Harm Reduction Coalition, accessed on January 18, 2019. harmreduction.org/about-us/principles-of-harm-reduction/.

32. Quoted in Elizabeth Hartney, "A Guide to DSM 5 Criteria for Substance Use Disorders," VeryWell, last updated September 26, 2018. www.verywellmind.com/dsm-5-criteria-for-substance-use-disorders-21926.

CHAPTER FIVE: ADDRESSING THE PROBLEM

33. "What Is Public Health," CDC Foundation, accessed on February 13, 2019. www.cdcfoundation.org/what-public-health.

34. Marianna Sotomayor, "Senate Passes Sweeping Legislation to Combat Opioid Epidemic," NBC, September 17, 2018. www.nbcnews.com/politics/politics-news/senate-passes-sweeping-legislation-combat-opioid-epidemic-n908901.

35. Quoted in Marianna Sotomayor, "Trump Signs Sweeping Opioid Bill with Vow to

End 'Scourge' of Drug Addiction," NBC, October 24, 2018. www.nbcnews.com/politics/congress/trump-signs-sweeping-opioid-bill-vow-end-scourge-drug-addiction-n923976.

36. Sotomayor, "Trump Signs Sweeping Opioid Bill."

GLOSSARY

blood alcohol concentration (BAC): The measure of the amount of alcohol in a person's system (also known as blood alcohol content). It is measured by grams of alcohol per deciliter of blood (g/dL).

collapsed vein: A condition that occurs when the inside lining of a vein is repeatedly damaged, eventually causing the sides of the vein to heal closed.

dependence: A condition that occurs when the body has started to physically rely on a drug to function.

harm reduction: A set of strategies that acknowledges the harm and tragic consequences of drug use and aims to reduce them as much as possible, while acknowledging that drug use is a reality and is not going to be completely stopped.

naloxone: A medication that quickly reverses the effects of an opioid overdose, allowing the person's respiratory functions to return to normal.

opioids: Drugs made from the poppy plant, including heroin, fentanyl, oxycodone, hydrocodone, morphine, and codeine.

overdose: The ingestion of more of a substance than the body can handle, which sometimes leads it to shut down.

perforated septum: A hole in the partition that divides the nostrils.

relapse: The use of drugs after a person has recovered or is in the process of recovery from a substance use disorder.

tolerance: A condition that occurs when the body has become used to a certain amount of a drug or alcohol and needs more to feel the same effects.

withdrawal: The symptoms that occur when a person cuts down on or completely quits the substance that they are addicted to.

ORGANIZATIONS TO CONTACT

Al-Anon Family Groups
1600 Corporate Landing Parkway
Virginia Beach, VA 23454
al-anon.org
Instagram: alanon_wso
YouTube: Al-AnonWSO
This organization offers support and meetings for the family and friends of people who are addicted to alcohol.

Centers for Disease Control and Prevention (CDC)
www.cdc.gov
Instagram: cdcgov
Snapchat: CDC
YouTube: CDC
The CDC provides information and research on diseases and disorders, including substance use disorders.

National Suicide Prevention Lifeline
988
988lifeline.org
Instagram: 988lifeline
YouTube: 988Lifeline
Many people with a substance use disorder have thought about suicide as a way to end their struggle with addiction. This national phone number connects people with a counselor in their area so they can talk through these feelings and get advice on how to find treatment. The website includes options to chat online or via text.

Substance Abuse and Mental Health Services Administration (SAMHSA)
5600 Fishers Lane
Rockville, MD 20857
www.samhsa.gov
Instagram: samhsagov
YouTube: SAMHSA
SAMHSA provides information on substance abuse and the mental health issues that may contribute to substance use disorders. The organization also includes information to help people with a substance use disorder find support and treatment.

FOR MORE INFORMATION

BOOKS

Bean, Cara. *Here I Am, I Am Me: An Illustrated Guide to Mental Health.* New York, NY: Workman Publishing, 2024.

Chambers, James. *PTSD and Coping with Trauma Information for Teens.* New York, NY: Omnigraphics, 2024.

Eason, Sarah, and Karen Latchana Kenney. *Having a Drug Addiction: Stories from Survivors.* Shropshire, UK: Cheriton Children's Books, 2022.

McKinney, Donna B. *Substance Addiction.* Minnesota, MN: ABDO Publishing Company, 2021.

Mooney, Carla. *Thinking Critically: Addiction.* San Diego, CA: ReferencePoint Press, 2023.

Smith, Elliott. *The Opioid Epidemic and the Addiction Crisis.* Minneapolis, MN: Lerner Publications, 2022.

WEBSITES

Mayo Clinic

www.mayoclinic.org

The Mayo Clinic has information on substance use disorders, including how to recognize the signs and how someone can get treatment for themselves or a loved one.

The Mighty: Addiction

themighty.com/topic/addiction

The Mighty is a website that addresses various physical and mental health issues. Under the topic of addiction, visitors can find personal stories, tips for treating addiction, and encouragement from others who have gone through similar issues.

MPOWRD

www.mpowrd.org

This website offers peer-led support for teens who are suffering from a substance use disorder. It has information for parents or guardians, social media campaigns, and the 12 steps for healing.

National Institute on Drug Abuse (NIDA)

www.drugabuse.gov

This website includes information on various aspects of substance abuse, including dangers and treatment.

INDEX

A

abuse, 9, 21, 42, 47, 49
addiction, 26, 36, 37, 40, 51
  brains and, 6, 8–9, 24, 39, 41, 43–45
  risk factors, 42–43, 46, 47, 50, 78
  See also treatment
  See also under alcohol; cannabis/marijuana; cocaine; heroin; opioids
adrenaline, 24, 26
age, 42–43, 45
alcohol, 60, 74
  addiction, 6, 9, 11, 48, 65
  effects of, 11–15, 16, 44, 54, 57, 59
anxiety, 22, 36, 40, 44, 57, 69
  cause of substance use, 13, 21, 49, 72
appetite, 21, 34, 53, 55

B

brain, 37, 47, 49, 54, 61, 80
  chemicals, 13, 16–17, 57, 58, 59
  See also under addiction

C

cancer, 25, 34
cannabis/marijuana, 17, 18–23
  addiction to, 11, 18, 21, 45, 65
  effects of, 16–18, 54, 57, 59
  medical, 15, 18–19, 21–22, 24
  See also tetrahydrocannabinol

Centers for Disease Control and Prevention (CDC), 25, 70, 73–74
children/teens, 12–13, 15, 45–47, 49, 59. *See also under* statistics
cigarettes, 8, 24–27, 45
cocaine, 8, 21, 32, 68, 80
  addiction to, 11, 34, 39
  effects of, 16, 24, 35, 54, 79–80
  fillers, 30, 34
criminalization, 15, 18–22, 51, 74, 82–83

D

death, 22, 55
  alcohol, 15, 16, 25, 30, 54, 60
  from mixing drugs, 30, 31
  from overdose, 18, 23, 70
decision-making/judgment, 15, 52–53, 54, 55
depression, 40, 57, 59, 69
  cause of substance use, 49, 72, 81–82
detoxification, 68–69
Diagnostic and Statistical Manual of Mental Disorders, Fifth Edition (DSM-5), 65, 67–68
digestive system, 16, 29, 24, 35, 52, 55
dopamine, 13, 17, 43, 44
Drug Enforcement Administration, U.S., (DEA), 21, 40

E

employment, 50–51, 52, 53, 59, 67, 71
endorphins, 13
euphoria, 8, 29, 32, 34

F

fentanyl, 30, 31, 32, 75–76
fillers, 30, 34

G

genetics, 42, 59

H

hallucinations, 17, 22, 26, 36–37, 39, 65
harm reduction, 62–65
health effects of substances, 11, 15, 51, 62. *See also* brain; cancer; death; digestive system; heart; hepatitis C; HIV; immune system; perforated septums; respiratory system; veins; withdrawal
heart, 25, 29, 35, 39, 81
  alcohol, 16, 60
  blood pressure, 22, 24, 26, 55
hepatitis C, 35, 53, 84
heroin, 8, 21, 27–29, 30, 78
  addiction to, 11, 32, 39, 49
  health effects of, 16, 31, 80
  treatment, 24, 68, 82
homelessness, 9
HIV, 35, 53, 74, 78, 82, 84
hydrocodone, 31

I

ibogaine, 81–82
immune system, 35, 55
inequality, 49–51
injections, 28, 55–56, 58, 80
inpatient programs, 68, 71, 77

L

legislation, 19, 70, 75–78
lidocaine, 34
lysergic acid diethylamide (LSD), 21, 39–40

M

memory, 15–17, 25, 37, 45, 55, 79–81
mental health, 9, 44, 47, 48, 56–57, 67. *See also* anxiety; *Diagnostic and Statistical Manual of Mental Disorders, Fifth Edition*; depression; post-traumatic stress disorder; schizophrenia; therapy
methadone, 69
methamphetamine, 35–37, 54, 56
morphine, 27–28, 31

N

naloxone, 58, 64, 83
National Institute on Drug Abuse (NIDA), 9, 15–16, 18, 34, 46, 56–57
  addiction as disease, 6, 44
National Institutes of Health (NIH), 75
nausea/vomiting, 21, 22, 37, 55, 60, 61
nicotine, 24–26

O

opioids, 8, 22–24, 29, 65, 77, 82
  alternatives, 70, 75
  See also heroin; hydrocodone; methadone; morphine; naloxone; opium poppies; oxycodone
  See also under statistics
opium poppies, 27–28, 31, 33

outpatient programs, 68, 71
overdose, 22–23, 28–29, 32, 58, 61, 74. *See also under* death
oxycodone, 30, 31

P

pain management, 21, 23, 70, 78
paranoia, 18, 22, 36, 37, 57
perforated septums, 31, 35
pharmaceutical companies, 32, 79
post-traumatic stress disorder (PTSD), 21, 40, 49, 72
prescription medicines, 6, 16, 26, 59, 74
  overprescription, 32, 70, 78
  See also fentanyl; hydrocodone; morphine; opioids; oxycodone
prevention efforts, 45–47
prisons, 74, 83
propranolol, 80
public health, 19, 70, 73–75, 79

R

race, 63, 65
relapse, 9, 41–42, 48, 61, 63, 72, 82
respiratory system, 25, 29, 58, 60, 61

S

schizophrenia, 25–26, 59
school, 45, 46, 53, 67
seizures/epilepsy, 21–22, 55, 60, 69
serotonin, 13
skin, 36–37, 56
sleep, 15, 34, 36, 53, 55

socioeconomic status, 42, 48, 49–51, 63, 65, 76
spice, 22–23
statistics, 25, 49, 50, 74, 82, 84
  alcohol, 11, 12–13, 54
  cannabis, 17, 18
  children/teens, 18, 32, 47, 50
  opioids, 32, 70, 78
stigma, 6, 11, 48, 62, 82, 84
stress, 42, 44, 45, 47, 49–50, 59
suicide, 61
support system, 9, 41, 55, 62, 63, 71

T

teeth, 35, 37, 56
tetrahydrocannabinol (THC), 15–17
therapy, 68, 71, 78, 83
tobacco, 24, 26–27, 65
tolerance, 14, 43, 51, 61, 67
  prescription medications, 8–9, 32, 78
trauma, 9, 40, 47, 49, 65
treatment, 9, 18, 49, 62–72, 74, 77. *See also* harm reduction; ibogaine; inpatient programs; methadone; naxalone; outpatient programs; therapy

V

vaping, 25, 26–27
veins, 55–56
violence, 36, 49, 53

W

withdrawal, 32, 44, 62, 67, 68–69, 82

PHOTO CREDITS

Cover, panitanphoto/Shutterstock.com; cover, pp. 1-104 Trisno Wardana/Shutterstock.com; cover, pp. 1,3, 4, 6, 11, 41, 52, 62, 73, 85, 91, 93, 95, 97, 103, 104 Sentavio/Shutterstock.com; p. 7 Di Studio/Shutterstock.com; p. 8 Andrew Angelov/Shutterstock.com; p. 12 Dr Faulkner/Shutterstock.com; p. 14 fiphoto/Shutterstock.com; p. 20 Canna Obscura/Shutterstock.com; p. 23 https://commons.wikimedia.org/wiki/File:JBMHH_substance_abuse_coordinator_warns_of_Spice_dangers_151022-A-DZ999-972.jpg; p. 25 Hazem.m.kamal/Shutterstock.com; p. 30 Joaquin Corbalan P/Shutterstock.com; p. 33 subcontinental/Shutterstock.com; p. 38 Featureflash Photo Agency/Shutterstock.com; p. 42 olgsera/Shutterstock.com; p. 44 chaiyo12/Shutterstock.com; p. 45 Halil ibrahim mescioglu/Shutterstock.com; p. 46 AstroStar/Shutterstock.com; p. 48 Kathy Hutchins/Shutterstock.com; p. 53 BongkarnGraphic/Shutterstock.com; p. 54 Gorodenkoff/Shutterstock.com; p. 58 EWY Media/Shutterstock.com; p. 60 Impact Photography/Shutterstock.com; p. 64 New2me86/Shutterstock.com; p. 66 LightField Studios/Shutterstock.com; p. 69 SCOOTERCASTER/Shutterstock.com; p. 72 wavebreakmedia/Shutterstock.com; p. 76 Andrei Minsk/Shutterstock.com; p. 77 Bill Perry/Shutterstock.com; p. 79 Bilbo Baggins/Shutterstock.com; p. 81 010110010101101/Shutterstock.com; p. 83 Jenari/Shutterstock.com.

ABOUT THE AUTHOR

SIMON PIERCE grew up in Jamestown, New York. He later moved to New York City and completed his education at NYU. He now lives in Brooklyn with his partner and their son. He has written for various health and wellness publications over the past seven years. He and his family enjoy people-watching in the park or reading the names on cemetery headstones and inventing stories about them.